SUCCESSFUL SCHOOL ADMINISTRATION

SUCCESSFUL SCHOOL ADMINISTRATION

By

Dr. Marlow Ediger
Professor Emeritus
Division of Education
Truman State University
P.O. Box 417, 201 W, 22nd St
North Newton KS 67117
United States of America

Dr. Digumarti Bhaskara Rao
M.Sc., M.A., M.A., M.Ed., Ph.D.
Reader
R.V.R. College of Education
Srinivasa Nagar Colony
Guntur–522 006
&
Member
Board of Studies in Education
Acharya Nagarjuna University
Nagarjuna Nagar
Andhra Pradesh
(India)

DISCOVERY PUBLISHING HOUSE
NEW DELHI-110002

First Published - 2006

Reprinted - 2016

ISBN: 978-81-8356-046-7

Successful School Administration

Published by:

DISCOVERY PUBLISHING HOUSE PVT. LTD.

4383/4B, Ansari Road, Darya Ganj

New Delhi-110 002 (India)

Phone: +91-11-23279245, 43596064-65

Fax: +91-11-23253475

E-mail: discoverypublishinghouse@gmail.com

sales@discoverypublishinggroup.com

web: www.discoverypublishinggroup.com

Printed at:

Infinity Imaging Systems

Delhi

Dedicated

To

Mr. B. Timmaiah

Founder & Correspondent
Adarsha Family of Educational Institutions
Sri Saraswathi College of Education, Ananthapur
Adarsha College of Education, Giddalur
Sri Sankara's College of Education, Kurnool
Andhra Pradesh

Mr. K. Tulasi Vishnu Prasad

Director & Correspondent
Sri Rama Educational Institutions
A.N.G. Ranga College of Education
K.M.M.R. Institute of Elementary Teacher Education
Chilumuru, Guntur, District: (A.P.)

Preface

School education is very crucial in the whole system of education in any country. School education prepares the future citizens and requires effective administration for its success. The duties of school education are going enormously day-by-day. Similarly, the responsibilities of a school administrator have grown by leaps and bounds in recent years. More is expected of school administrators than ever before and the chances of there responsibilities will increase rapidly in this technological era.

The contents of this book on successful school administration will provide the school administrator practical and theoretical ideas in administering a quality school.

Marlow Ediger
Bhaskara Rao

Sai Soudha
D-43, S.V.N. Colony
Guntur, 522 006
Andhra Pradesh

Contents

1

Administration in Education

Each administrator selects and implements selected philosophical strands of thought in the decision-making arena. A single school of philosophy may be followed. Or, an eclectic approach might be utilised in that several philosophical schools of thought are inherent to make decisions. Whichever means are used, each decision made rests upon philosophy more so than objectivity or empirical means.

Realism and the Curriculum

A realist administrator advocates that faculty members state objectives in measurable terms. The instructor then chooses learning activities for learners to attain the precise ends. After instruction, the instructor measures if specific objectives have been attained. If attained, learners individually are ready to move on to the next sequential end. New learning activities might be necessary for unsuccessful learners in goal attainment.

Realists believe to objective, real world can be known by learners as it truly is. Thus, goals can be selected which are objective, independent of any observer. The personal feelings and values of instructors must be minimised in choosing objectives for learner attainment, according to realists. There are objectives which need discovering. The objectives represent reality as it is and as it exists. Personal biases and prejudices have no room in a realist's curriculum. The ends of instruction, then, are truly objective. After instruction, the instructor may measure if goal attainment has occurred. Measurement results are obtained objectively, regardless of personal perceptions possessed by appraiser.

The scientific, objective world is reality for realists. Thus, science and mathematics become highly significant curriculum areas. Natural phenomena are observable and describable. There, of course, are new discoveries in the world of science. Human beings continually need to learn more about nature and its laws. New phenomena must be continually discovered in the real world of science. Mathematics is orderly, precise, and is the language of science.

Other curriculum areas also contain precise, objective subject matter. These include history (accurately described names, dates, places, and events are in evidence), geography (precise geographical phenomena, such as plains, plateaus, hills, rivers, valley, and lakes, among others), grammar and usage (sentence patterns and methods of expanding sentences are describable) and political science (describable governmental institutions). Even standards of morality that have stood the test of time, may be objectified as they exist in society.

Realist administrators may tend to deemphasise:

1. general objectives in teaching-learning situations;
2. subjective knowledge consisting of opinions and feelings of individuals and groups;
3. ideas that cannot be tested in a laboratory or societal setting;
4. pupil-teacher planning in which processes are stressed to the exclusion of objective products.

Experimentalism and the Curriculum

Experimentalists believe in a continually changing environment. Since scenes and situations change, new problems arise. The problems need identification. Related data or information need to be acquired. After which, a hypothesis needs developing in answer to the problematic situation. The hypothesis needs testing in society. If evidence warrants, the hypothesis should be revised. Otherwise, it may be utilised again in a new problematic situation.

Society definitely does not stay stable or static, but *change* is a key concept in experimentalist thinking. Effort or purpose is perceived by learners as they sense reasons for identifying and solving problems. Interest is then inherent in learning. Interest brings forth and is not separated from effort.

What is reality in the world of experimentalism is that which can be experienced. The learner cannot know the real world objectively as it truly is, according to experimentalists. One, however, can *experience* social and natural phenomena.

School and society should not be separated entities. Thus, problem, issues, and trends in society become subject matter for learner acquisition. Subject matter is instrumental to the solving of problems. It is definitely not an end, in and of itself.

Experimentalists tend to deemphasise the following in the curriculum:

1. subject matter learned for its own sake. Rather, subject matter needs to be gained to solve relevant societal problems;
2. drill and practice in the curriculum;
3. dividing the curriculum into specific academic areas. Subject matter becomes significant in problem solving. Whatever content is needed is used, regardless of which academic are is important at a given time. Thus, in all reality, academic areas lose their boundaries and borders;
4. teachers selecting objectives, learning activities, and evaluation procedures. Rather pupils must be guided to identify and solve problems. Learner, rather than sole teacher purpose is important in the curriculum;
5. individual decisions rather than committee endeavours. In society, committees identify and attempt to solve problems. Thus, pupils in committees need to be involved in problems solving activities.

Existentialism and the Curriculum

Existentialists administrators believe in the individual, himself/herself, making choices and decisions. There are no ethical or moral guidelines that are absolutes. The person must develop quality criteria to follow in life.

These standards should not come from other human beings, nor from the infinite. To have others make choices for the personal self makes one less than human. To be human means to choose and to make decisions. The chooser, alone, is responsible for choices made. No other being can or must assume the consequences of personal decisions made.

Each person then must make moral choices in a complete atmosphere of freedom. Choices are made in an irrational, not a rational environment. Dread and anxiety may be inherent in making these decisions. Choices made can well make for feelings of awe. The consequences of a choice may result in alienation and not necessarily in feelings of friendship and happiness.

Existentialists administrators frown upon the following:

1. the teacher choosing objectives, learning activities and evaluation procedures with little or no learner involvement;
2. large group instruction and committee work emphasis with little or no learner decision-making;
3. rote learning and memorisation of subject matter;
4. objective academic area (science and mathematics, in particular) emphasis with a deemphasis upon subjective content (art, music, literature and drama);
5. measurably stated predetermined objectives for learner attainment.

Idealism and the Curriculum

Idealist administrators believe that ideas pertaining to the natural and social world can be known. The real world as it truly is content be known. An idea centred curriculum then becomes important.

Human beings are finite, limited individuals. A quality subject centred curriculum may guide learners continually to move in the direction of the infinite. Which subject matter areas should provide learners an idea centred curriculum?

Subject matter chosen should represent stability of content. Continuously changing ideas do not represent the stableness that idealists seek. Subject matter chosen for pupil learning needs to represent universality of ideas. Thus, relevant learnings are significant, not only for the present, but also have endured in space and time. What is important to learn has stood the test of time within universal geographical regions.

A study of history and geography has been important for educated people through the ages and should guide learners to achieve in the direction of the infinite. Mathematics has relevant generalisations and universal ideas for learner attainment. To be able to express oneself in a less finite way, the language arts areas of listening, speaking, reading and writing become highly significant. Universal subject matter in science and health might also assist learners to achieve worthwhile content in moving away from being finite and in the direction of the infinite.

Idealists tend to frown at the following in the curriculum:

1. subject matter that is in a state of flux and continual revision;
2. specific facts which do not relate to broader generalisations and universal application;
3. recent literature in diverse academic areas to the exclusion of worthwhile enduring ideas of the past;
4. subject matter studied to solve problems only, to the exclusion of attaining content for its own sake;
5. emphasis placed upon objects and the objective world of science and mathematics to the exclusion of enduring content in the social sciences, the humanities, and the fine arts.

What is relevant to idealists is (a) universal, not specific; (b) stable, not transitory; (c) abstract, not concrete; and (d) not easily observable, but needs depth seeking and searching.

In Summary

Each administrator adheres to selected principles, rules, and generalisations in the making of decisions. Thus, guidance and direction provides impetus in making choices in school and in society.

Administrators need to study and appraise diverse philosophical schools of thought in the philosophical domain. Ultimately, choices need to be made as to which philosophical school(s) of thought harmonises best with the perception of the decision-maker in the curriculum.

2

Issues in School Administration

There are selected issues in administration which need attempts at synthesis. Which issues then might be studied, analysed, and resolved?

Role of thc Administrator

There are numerous roles performed by individuals in school administration. A major dichotomy pertains to be the degree that administrators should be involved in curriculum improvement. Toward one end of the continuum, an administrator may continually be talking with diverse teachers involving recent trends in curriculum development. The trends, among others, might include programmed learning, inductive methods of teaching, use of learning centres, instructional management systems and mastery learning, Individually Prescribed Instruction (IPI), individualised reading, non-graded schools, team teaching, Peer Mediated Instruction (PMI), and Management by Objective (MBO). The administrator might encourage teacher involvement in workshops and faculty meetings pertaining to each of the above named innovative means of instruction. The school administrator may also visit teachers to observe actual teaching, followed by a conference with that involved teacher. Routine administrative is completed prior to and after any given school day.

Toward the other end of the continuum, an administrator may believe that quality teachers were hired initially and each will be motivated to do the best possible to provide for individual differences among learners. This administrator may well leave curriculum matters in the hands of teachers. He/she rather will supervise custodial services to notice if a school building is kept adequately tidy for pupil learning. Also, the administrator here encourages a cafeteria/lunch room situation in which learners have wholesome eating quarters together with proper manners displayed. The administrator might also notice that school repairs are made when necessary, as well as learner permanent records are kept accurately and comprehensively. Additional responsibilities might include:

1. answering all/most telephone calls personally;
2. attempting to be entirely responsible for the public relations domain;
3. conveying messages by telephone to parents and other interested parties;
4. typing, in degrees, all correspondence involving patrons in the community, as well as with the business world.

As a model, Knezevich wrote the following possible contributions of administrators:

- Exists to implement the decisions of a legislative body.
- Influences the results to be achieved, the direction to be pursued and the priorities to be recognised within the enterprise.
- Has a decisive impact on strategies selected and utilised to reach predetermined objectives.
- Determining, in large measure, the organisational climate and working relationships.
- Can help to make personnel employed more productive (or, when it falters, less effective).
- Helps to assemble and to insure prudent use of resources.
- Unifies and coordinates the human and material resources available to the enterprise.
- Appraises the quality and quantity of outcomes actually accomplished.

- Shapes, to a considerable degree, the image and prestige of the enterprise.

Activity-centred Versus Subject-centred Curriculum

Should learners be active or passive beings in the curriculum? There are selected administrators who believe in an activity, centred curriculum. Thus, pupils with teacher guidance plan, implement, and evaluate diverse ongoing and completed projects. These projects might involve:

1. art experiences;
2. construction work;
3. processing materials;
4. dramatic activities;
5. work with puppets and marionettes;
6. music and rhythmic experiences;
7. excursions;
8. simulation and games.

Administrators emphasising an activity centred curriculum emphasise the following philosophical beliefs:

1. pupils need to be involved in making curricular decisions;
2. subject matter is not learned for its own sake, but rather as a means to an end, such as gathering information to participate in an activity or complete a project;
3. interests of learners can be developed and maintained if pupils are actively involved in learning;
4. purpose is involved in learning if pupils make choices and decisions;
5. meaningful learnings accrue if pupils accept that which is being planned and completed in terms of projects and activities.

Administrators in schools reveal preferences for either an activity-centred or subject-centred curriculum through verbal and nonverbal cues.

Administrators advocating a subject-centred curriculum believe that essential, basic ideas for learners to attain exist in reputable textbooks, library books, encyclopaedias, and other vital reference sources. Subject matter that has endured in space and time in preferred to that which changes rather continuously and is subject to modification. Thus, pupils need to acquire subject matter to become proficient citizens in society at a later time. The teacher needs to stimulate pupils to become motivated learners. Quality teaching may bring forth relevant ideas involving essential subject matter.

Who do selected administrators emphasise pupils learning significant, enduring subject matter?

1. The learner presently needs to acquire much subject matter in order to use, as an adult, what has been learned previously.
2. Learners need to be relatively passive in nature to achieve worth-while content. Self-discipline and obedience are desired traits which might be developed as a result of studying subject matter.
3. Relevant ideas are recorded in reputable textbooks and other printed materials. Thus, trivia is minimised in ongoing units of study involving subject matter content.
4. Stability of subject matter in the curriculum is to be desired, as compared to projects/activities which are transitory, unimportant, and changing.
5. Adult minds are in a better position to determine relevancy in the curriculum, as compared to the thoughts, ideas, and wishes of learners.

Salzer and Drdek wrote the following involving open-ended standard forms of schooling:

The most significant differences between open, or informal, approaches and standard forms of schooling have to do with the matter of choice on the part of pupils. In the traditional school nearly all decisions have been made by the teacher or the teacher's superiors, while in informally organised classes children have a substantial degree of control over learning activities and the conditions governing their work.

In the open classroom pupils do not have, absolute, freedom, of course, for the teacher represents society's interest in seeing that the basic skills are learned, knowledge gained, and positive attitudes developed. But the informal-classroom teacher recognises that children learn in many ways and that learning may proceed better if the pupils have some control over their time schedules and the physical space and facilities of the room.

Which children have the opportunity to choose among alternatives and receive guidance in making the choices most appropriate to their developmental levels, they grow in that ability. In the open classroom, pupils are typically given some control over the disposition of time, with occasional interventions by the teacher. The child's daily or weekly schedule may include regular commitments, with other segments planned cooperatively by pupils and teacher. For a significant portion of the hours spent in school, however, the pupil has the responsibility of deciding how to use the available time to meet the teacher's expectations and his or here goals.

Administration: Art or Science

There are selected educators who believe that administration of schools is an art, and not a science. Thus, the administrator create his/her own roles in the school setting. Creativity is a key concept to emphasise when advocating administration as being an art. Tiedt and Tiedt listed the following characteristics of creative beings:

1. Nonconformity of ideas, but not necessarily of dress and behaviour.
2. Egotism and feelings of destiny.
3. Great curiosity, desire to discover the answer.
4. Sense of humour and playfulness.
5. Perseverance on self-started projects.

6. Intense emotions, sincerity.
7. Tendency to be shy.
8. Lack of rigidity.

In being a creative person, the administrator realises that no absolute or formal standards exist which must be followed to be a quality leader. Rather open ended situations are in evidence. Flexibility is a key concept to follow. Authoritarianism as a concept is to be frowned upon. The school administrator develops new hypotheses and tests them in contextual situations. Feedback is then obtained to notice now successful implemented decisions were in improving the curriculum.

There are numerous means available to an administrator to improve the curriculum. Among others, the following are possibilities:

1. workshops and faculty meetings for faculty members;
2. teachers visiting innovative classrooms;
3. video-taping teaching performance and providing feedback to the involved teacher;
4. teachers on a given grade level cooperatively developing resource units to be used in the class setting;
5. faculty members involved in taking teaching performance tests.

In each of the above named plans of inservice education, there are no definite standards to follow. The creative administrator then realises that administration is an art rather than a science. There are, however, selected broad guidelines for the administrator to follow. These might include:

1. guiding faculty members to perceive purpose in inservice education programmes;
2. assisting teachers to implement into classroom teaching salient concepts and generalisations achieved through inservice education;

3. helping teachers to engage in self-appraisal in ongoing units of study involving teaching and learning;
4. guiding faculty members in selecting learning activities which truly provide for individual differences among learners.

Ediger wrote the following pertaining to a model workshop, as one example, involving inservice education.

1. The theme of the social studies workshop should be decided upon cooperatively by the participants. Thus, relevant themes may include (a) implementing recommended trends in teaching elementary school social studies, (b) using inquiry approaches in teaching social studies, (c) developing teaching units and resource units, (d) using problem solving approaches in teaching-learning situations, (e) providing for individual differences in reading social studies content, (f) implementing concepts pertaining to nongradedness and open space education, (g) using team teaching in the social studies, (h) updating procedures to evaluate pupil achievement, and (i) utilising appropriate sequential learning experiences in the social studies.
2. The general session should be utilised to help participants identify relevant problems in teaching social studies. Thus, teachers may identify such relevant problems as: (a) stimulating pupil interest in the social studies, (b) guiding the slow learner in achieving in his optimum, (c) developing meaningful tasks for pupils in open space education, (d) planning objectives, learning experiences, and evaluation procedures cooperatively in a true team teaching situation, (e) coping with discipline problems in the class setting, (f) helping the disadvantaged child, and (g) making teaching aids to provide for individual differences in the social studies.

3. Committees should be formed to work on problems identified in the general session. Committee membership should (a) be voluntary, (b) meet the needs of participations, and (c) help individuals to solve problems in teaching social studies.
4. Individual study in necessary in providing for individual differences among participants in the workshop. Individuals may work in the direction of solving problems pertaining to: (a) selecting relevant social studies units, (b) choosing social studies textbooks and other reading materials appropriate for a given set of learners, (c) evaluating the current social studies programme in terms of criteria, and (d) maintaining an updated social studies curriculum.

The above named criteria must be considered in a flexible manner. Thus, considerable leeway exists for administrators being truly creative in developing the curriculum.

Toward the other end of the spectrum, there are selected educators advocating that education is a science, rather than an art. The administrator's goal is to guide teachers to write objectives in teaching in measurable terms. Perhaps, the administrator believes strongly in mastery learning. Thus, objectives may need to be written in measurable terms at least on semester, prior to their implementation in classroom teaching. The ends are arranged hierarchically in a sequential manner. Each pupil needs to attain a minimal number of objectives before being promoted to the next grade level. Or, a selected number of ends must be achieved before successfully completing a semester, or entire course.

The teacher selects vital learning activities to guide learners to attain a specific end. If a pupil is successful in goal attainment, he/she may then achieve the next sequential end. If a student did not attain an objective, he/she may need a different instructional strategy to achieve that same goal. Only, if an objective is maintained may the learner progress to the next sequential goal.

James Popham emphasises the following criteria for administrators in supervising of teachers who utilise measurable stated objectives:

Function One: A criterion-referenced instructional supervisor must help the teacher select more defensible educational objectives. The supervisor and teacher:

1. identify any curricular constraints;
2. state all objectives operationally;
3. consider alternative objectives;
4. evaluate and decide on each potential objective.

Function Two: A criterion-referenced supervisor assists the teacher in achieving the teacher's instructional objectives.

The supervisor:

1. determines the teachers objectives;
2. secures evidence regarding their achievement;
3. looks for undesirable side effects;
4. suggests alternative procedures for unachieved objectives.

Grouping Pupils for Instruction

Any administrator is faced with the problem of how to group learners for teaching and learning. There are numerous possibilities. Each plan has its pros and cons.

One issue pertains to homogeneous versus heterogeneous grouping. In homogeneous grouping in any curriculum area, pupils are as alike as possible in knowledge and skills possessed. Uniformity is then wanted in terms of understandings and abilities possessed. It might be easier for a teacher to plan objective, learning activities, an evaluation procedures if a class is relatively similar in academic progress. Many teachers find it difficult to provide for individual differences if a wide range of achievement among learners is in evidence in a classroom.

Toward the other end of the continuum, selected administrators favour heterogeneous grouping. Learners in a class then process mixed progress levels. The range of achievement might be from below average, to average, to talented learners all being taught in one classroom. In society, individuals interact with others regardless of ability levels. This is a necessity when taking care of personal and social needs in life's settings, outside the local school environment.

Ragan and Shepherd iisted the following advantages and disadvantages of homogeneous as well as heterogeneous grouping:

Advantages Claimed for Homogeneous Grouping

1. The teacher who has a group of abler pupils can challenge these pupils to work up to their capacity by using more difficult materials, excepting them to progress more rapidly from one level of difficulty to another, and requiring a higher quality of performance.
2. The teacher who has a group of less capable pupils can gear the instruction to their level of ability by using easier materials, giving them more time to progress from one level of difficulty to another, and setting more realistic standards for performance.
3. Differentiated instruction in terms of ability and effort enhance equality of opportunity for pupils with wide variations in ability.
4. Parents, especially those whose children are in the upper ability group, generally favour the plan.
5. Teachers, who are inclined to hope that some plan will be found to give them a group of pupils who are somewhat alike in ability, generally favour the plan.
6. It is more true to life to have pupils compete with those who are somewhere near their own level of ability; slow pupils particularly have better opportunities to become leaders in their own groups.
7. Teachers have an opportunity to do a better job of teaching the skill subjects when the pupils in their classes do not vary so widely in ability.

8. The teacher has a better opportunity to work with individuals when the range of ability in the class is reduced somewhat.

Limitations Claimed for Homogeneous Grouping

1. Grouping pupils into high, average, and low groups does not significantly reduce variations among the pupils in these groups: teachers must still provide differentiated instruction within these groups.
2. The plan will not accomplish the purpose of providing instruction for each pupil according to his ability unless the materials provided for each group are suitable for pupils of that general level of ability; this is not always done.
3. The plan violates the pupils' right to be different; when they are labelled slow, average, or bright, they begin to think of themselves in these terms and begin to try to be like others in their group.
4. The plan pays little attention to any characteristic of a pupil other than the trait used the basis for grouping; there is evidence that pupils with similar scores on intelligence tests may differ widely with respect to other characteristics.
5. It is difficult to find teachers who are willing to work only with slow groups.
6. Ability grouping is a form of segregation; the pupils in the high ability group generally come from families at the higher socioeconomic level.
7. Parents frequently object having their children assigned to the slow group.
8. There is no evidence to support the contention that higher achievement occurs as a result of homogeneous grouping.

Advantages Claimed for Heterogeneous Grouping

1. The interaction of the various ability levels contributes to development and achievement.

2. Heterogeneous groups are more like the relationships in life.
3. The models and alternatives available to pupils and teachers are more numerous.
4. Some research studies generally favour social, affective, and maturational advantages for children in heterogeneous groups.

Disadvantages Claimed for Heterogeneous Grouping

1. The research evidence concerning achievement generally suggests that there is no difference between the two grouping plans.
2. The wider range of variations in achievement needs and capacities makes it difficult for the teacher to provide for the individualisation of instruction.
3. The pupils who learn more slowly are less likely to have opportunities for leadership and success because of the presence of quicker pupils.

Other issue involved in grouping pertain to the pros and cons of:

1. team teaching;
2. the nongraded school;
3. interage grouping;
4. the dual progress plan;
5. learning centres and open spaces;
6. computer assisted instruction.

Marking and Reporting Learner Progress

How should pupils be graded in school work? There are selected administrators who believe that students would be graded in terms of effort put forth. Thus, a slow learner might receive the top grades given if he/she achieves optimally, regardless of ability levels. Average and talented achievers, of course, may also receive the best grades given if they achieve as well as possible, individually. Conversely, slow, average, and fast learners might receive lower grades, if effort is lacking.

Toward the other end of the continuum, certain administrators advocate giving top achievers A grades, less effective achievers B grades, while the remainder might receive C, D, or even F grades, depending upon achievement. Thus, regardless of abilities possessed, pupils might be graded on what would be called a bell shaped curve. Thus, there will be a few A grades given, slightly more B grades, the majority will receive C grades, followed by students who receive D grades being equal in number, approximately, to those receiving B grades. A few receive F grades. The distribution of grades may well represent the normal distribution curve, also called the bell-shaped curve.

There are selected schools utilising both philosophies of grading, e.g. grading learners in terms of effort put forth as well as being compared with other classmates in terms of academic achievement.

Which means should be used to report pupil progress to parents? The report card is an older method in reporting learner achievement. One problem among others, pertains to how many categories in any one curriculum area, should parents know about pupil achievement. For example, in the curriculum area of reading, a single grade of A, B, C, D or F could be recorded by the teacher for each pupil. A question might then arise pertaining to the meaning of that single letter grade. Are there component analysed parts which make up the reading curriculum? The answer definitely is *yes*. Thus, the following categories in word recognition could appear in a report card in reporting pupil progress in the curriculum area of reading:

1. phonetic analysis or phonics
2. syllabication
3. structural analysis
4. picture clues
5. context clues
6. configuration clues.

In addition to word recognition techniques, comprehension skills, as categories could also appear on report cards to report pupil progress to parents. These include:

1. reading to acquire facts
2. scanning or skimming
3. gaining sequential ideas
4. acquiring main ideas
5. reading critically
6. creative reading
7. recreational reading
8. reading to solve problem.

The above named categories in word recognition and comprehension involve the curriculum area of reading only. There are numerous other academic areas which need to appear on report cards to report pupil progress to pertains. There are definite questions which might be asked pertaining to a categories approach in reporting learner progress to parents. These include:

1. What would be a reasonable number of categories on a report card for teachers to assess learner progress in?
2. How many specific categories evaluated might parents truly understand in how well their offspring are doing?
3. Are parents able to attach meaning to each category, when a realistic number appear on a report card?

A major problem then pertains to a reasonable number of categories for teachers to mark to report learner progress to parents, as well as a reasonable number which parents understand in realising how well their child is progressing in schools.

Additional issues in reporting learner progress to parents involve:

1. How should parent-teacher conferences be conducted to truly work in the direction in offering the best curriculum possible for each student?

2. When might the telephone be utilised to report learner progress to parents.
3. Might the writing of letters parents assist in clarifying how wall a learner is doing in the school/ class setting.

In Summary

There are diverse issues that need resolving as to the duties and responsibilities of administrator. Each role needs to be analysed. Attempt then need to be made to synthesise that which is unresloved. Exemplorary role models need developing which assist teachers to achieve optimally. Each teacher needs to select the best in terms of objectives, learning activities, and evaluation procedures for individual learners.

Diverse philosophies in education need to be studied. Ultimately, the philosophy or philosophies adopted should guide in developing a curriculum which provides for interests, needs, and purpose of each student.

REFERENCES

Ediger, Marlow, *The Elementary Curriculum, A Handbook*, Kirksville, Missouri: Simpson Publishing Company, 1977, Pages 133-134.

Knezevich, Stephen J., *Administration of Public Education*, Third Edition. New York: Harper and Row Publishers, 1975, Page 3.

Popham, James, *Instructional Supervision, A Criterion-Referenced Strategy*. Los Angelos: Vimcet Associates, 1969, Filmstrip and Tape.

Ragan, William and Shepherd, Gene, *Modern Elementary Curriculum*. Fifth Edition. New York: Holt, Rinehart, and Winston, 1977, Pages 125-127.

Salzer, Richard T., and Drdek, Richard E., "Organising for Learning," in Walter T. Petty (Editor). *Curriculum for the Modern Elementary School*. Chicago: Rand McNally College Publishing Company, 1976, pages 58-59.

Tiedt, Iris M., and Tiedt, Lowell, *Contemporary English in the Elementary School*, Second Edition. Englewood Cliffs, New Jersey: Prentice-Hall, Inc., 1975, Page 151.

3

Philosophy of Education and the School Administrator

Each school administrator functions in terms of following selected philosophies of education. A philosophy gives guidance and direction to the involved administrator. Which philosophies might be relevant for school administrators to analyse or adopt?

Realism and the Curriculum

A school administrator, following tenets of realism, generally believes that one can know the real natural and social world as it truly is. Thus, a replica of the environment can be obtained by the observer. The real world exists independently of the observer.

Since the real world can be known as it exists, the realists administrator may believe in using measurably stated objectives in teaching and learning. Thus, what exists can be identified and measured rather precisely. Science and mathematics content in particular, are specific. Other curriculum areas, such as history, geography, literature, and even values have objective content which has stood the test of time and is prized highly.

After precise of objectives have been selected by the teacher, learning activities need choosing to guide each pupil to achieve chosen goals. Each learner's prógress may then be evaluated in terms of the measurable objectives.

A school administrator emphasising realism, as a philosophy of education may also believe in Management by

Objective (MBO). Measurable objectives are then selected cooperatively by administrators and teachers. The chosen ends are identified at the beginning of a new school year. As the school year progresses, administrators and teachers need to evaluate if adequate progress is being made in attaining the desired ends. Definite means need to be in evidence to achieve the measurable objectives. If the precise ends are not being achieved as the school year progresses, reasons need to be found for the identified deficiencies. Perhaps, new approaches need to trying to attain desired cbjectives goals. The real world may then be identified and reorganised as it truly is. Objectivity is highly relevant to realists.

Idealism and the Curriculum

An administrator following tenets of idealism, as a philosophy of education, believes in an idea centred curriculum. Thus, one can not know the real world as it truly is. However, the perceiver receives ideas relating to what has been observed, read, and written.

Idealist administrators are strong believers in a quality general education curriculum for learners. Literature, grammar, spelling, history, geography, mathematics, and science, in particular, provide necessary learnings for pupils in moving away from being finite individuals to becoming infinite.

Universal ideas need acquiring by pupils. The universal ideas are relevant regardless of space or time of the involved learner. Universals remain rather stable are not subject to continuous change. The learners perception of worthwhile universal ideas, however, may change.

Vocational education during the elementary and secondary school years have little or no value to an idealist. Vocational goals can be stressed beyond the second y years of schooling. A subject centred curriculum is relevant for pupils, according to idealists. Vital ideas might then be acquired in moving in the direction of the infinite.

Existentialism and the Curriculum

Existentialists believe that individuals, not groups, choose their own goals in life. Life is absurd and ridiculous. Within these situations, each person needs to develop personal meanings and values in life. Goals are not given to any person. The ends and means of living must be sought. Making moral decisions on an individual basis is central to the thinking of existentialists. Each person is responsible for decisions made. Other human beings or God cannot be blamed for the outcomes of personal decision-making. Awesome responsibilities are involved when each moral decision is made.

Existentialist administrators may well encourage each teacher to choose highly flexible objective, learning activities, and evaluation procedures. The individual teacher is challenged to develop moral decisions and accept the consequences of choices made. To develop existentialist pupils, the teacher must permit learners on an individual basis to choose ends, means, and appraisal procedures within, flexible limits. Pupils need to be guided to realise the world is not rational. However, each pupil must accept the consequences of personal choices made. Thus, immense responsibilities rest upon each pupil as to decisions made in the school curriculum, as well as in the curriculum of life.

Experimentalism and the Curriculum

Experimentalists believe the world of experience to represent ultimate reality. One can know that which is experienced only. The natural/social environment changes rather continuously. New problems then arise. These problems must be identified and solved. Groups, not involved, must identify and solve related problems. Effort to solve problems comes from being interested in ongoing experiences and activities.

Experimentalist administrators emphasise working with teachers cooperatively to truly choose and resolve problems in the schools and class setting. Administrators alone, definitely should not identify and solve problems. Problems and solutions will not remain stable, for change in the school environment is continually in evidence. Curriculum and discipline problems need identification and viable solutions sought.

Pupils with teacher guidance need to identify questions and seek answers using a variety of learning activities in all curriculum areas. With pupil purpose involved in finding answers to questions and problems, effort, is put forth in learning. Interest in learning then provides needed effort. The teacher definitely should not lecture subject matter content to pupils. Rather, subject matter is useful in solving problems and answering questions.

In Closing

Administrators need to study and analyse diverse philosophies of education. Accepted philosophies may then be utilised to provide for individual differences among pupils. Each learner needs to perceive interest, purpose and motivation in learning. Optimal achievement may then be in evidence for each pupil.

4

Administration and the Curriculum

Who should be involved in making curricular decisions? There are diverse sources from which subject matter, ideas, and power might come in the decision-making arena.

Power Structure in the Curriculum

Expert power might provide impetus in attempting to solve problems in the curriculum. An administrator possessing expert power has needed understanding, skills, and attitudes in developing a quality school setting. Expert power might well include proficiency in maintaining positive discipline, adequate teaching materials and supplies, accepted means of inservice education of staff, quality custodial services, nutritious/appetizing food served in the lunchroom, positive relations with the school governing board, adequate funding for the school, and wholesome relations with the lay public.

Administrators possessing expert power are looked up to by faculty, staff, and other school workers as having leadership qualities which are truly conducive in achieving the best of objectives, learning activities, and appraisal procedures to guide optimal progress within each learner. Expert power is earned due to being a true professional. Facades are not needed. In his/her own right, the administrator possessing expert power possesses those qualities which are admirable in developing a relevant curriculum. The administrator then is an expert in the field of education. Other school workers intrinsically realise the effectiveness, efficiency and professionalism of administrators possessing expert power.

A second type of administrators might reflect charismatic power. He/she is able to influence others due to poise, polish and charm. School workers and the lay public and attracted to individuals possessing charisma. Seemingly charismatic administrators have the ability to attract others to do what is deemed necessary to improve the curriculum. Forcing others to accomplish and achieve is definitely not the role of a charismatic administrator. Rather, the involved administrator has mannerisms, behaviour, and approaches conductive to influencing others in a relaxed way.

Content revealed by the charismatic administrator may indicate expert knowledge, abilities and attitudes. However, more significant than expert power is a polished performance to influence listeners. A pleasant means in changing listeners' behaviour is then involved. A person possessing charisma tends to be an individual well liked by others.

A third type of administrator emphasises coercive power. Thus, an administrator is in a position to pressure teachers, aides, custodians, and lunchroom workers to conform. The coercive administrator has adequate status to secure obedience from others. Quality relevant ideals may or may not be expressed when forcing school personnel to be obedient.

Means of punishing disobedient behaviour are available and utilised to implement desire norms of the coercive administrator. Using charisma is definitely not a major goal in working with teachers and other school workers. Charismatic behaviour is utilised if it assists the administrator to be more forceful or powerful in pressuring others to adopt conformity behaviour.

A fourth type of administrative behaviour involves legitimate power. Administrators are licensed by an accrediting agency. The license based upon completing course work in an approved college/university and appropriate internships provides the administrator with legitimate power. Teachers and other school workers realise that administrators are certified to perform a professional leadership role. Thus, the administrator possesses a selected type of power legitimized by an accrediting agency. Legitimate power may not, by itself provide an adequate basis for teachers and other school workers to accept the leadership role of the administrator. No doubt other types of power will need to be added, such as expert knowledge. Legitimate power plus expert might well provide an administrator with quality leadership capabilities. Additional types of power, such as charisma, further enhances the administrator's abilities to become a proficient leader.

In Summary

Prospective administrators need to study and analyse diverse types of power in providing leadership in the school, class, and societal arena. Ultimately, an administrator needs to adopt strategies in which leadership may be provided to develop a quality curriculum to provide optimal learner progress.

5

Role of Administration in the Curriculum

There are diverse roles that administrators perform in the curriculum. Certainly, the overall goal of administration is to, improve the curriculum. To improve the curriculum, recommended guidelines need to be followed. Which criteria then should administrators follow?

The Administrators and the Curriculum

Innovations designed to strengthen the curriculum require dedicated leadership from the administrator. Thus, the administrator is a key individual to guide faculty members to make desired changes in the curriculum. To provide leadership, an administrator must be knowledgeable and skillful to lead faculty members to move from the present status quo to a desired norm. Objectives in the curriculum eventually provide the meter-stick against which all changes need evaluation. Cooperatively, faculty members with administrative leadership need to develop viable ends. Recommended standards need to be followed in developing desired objectives. Faculty members, with administrative leadership, need to have much input into developing the curriculum. The standards might well include the following:

1. each participant must actively participate in diverse sessions devoted to improving the curriculum;
2. no one should dominate any one committee session;

3. the administrator needs to encourage *all* participants to participate;
4. ideas need to circulate within a committee, and not move between a participant and administrator only;
5. participants need to stay on the topic being pursued and not digress to other facets of information.

Objectives in the Curriculum

Administrators then have vital leadership roles in guiding faculty members to determines significant objectives. The agreed upon objectives must reflect that which is worthy for students to learn. Competent faculty members with administrative leadership must develop viable goals for student attainment. It is important for faculty members to weed out what is trivia and deadwood in each course offering.

The administrator must leave leeway for each faculty member to emphasise personal desired, philosophies in the teaching arena. These philosophies may include the following:

1. experimentalism, in which ultimate reality is represented by *experience*. *Change* is experienced by all. Thus, problems arise and need solutions;
2. idealism, in which *ideas* represent ultimate reality. One can know ideas but not the natural/social environment in and of itself. Relevant universal ideas need emphasis and not specifics in the curriculum. The universals tend to endure in time and space;
3. realism, in which the knower can know the natural/social environment as it truly is. Thus, precise, accurate knowledge may be known by the knower. Measurable objectives might be written for students to attain;
4. existentialism, in which the individual makes choices and decisions. The choices and decisions must be moral, and yet no guidelines exist as to what can be called morality. Truth then becomes subjective to the knowers. Individuals live in an irrational world.

Learning Activities and Evaluation Procedures

Administrators may provide leadership in being supportive to purchasing and utilising a variety of learning activities by involved instructors. Text-books need to be carefully evaluated and chosen. Additional learning activities to be utilised in classroom instruction include relevant films, film-strips, slides, tapes, records, and transparencies. Each learning activity emphasised in teaching and learning should guide learners to achieve viable objectives. Student questions and comments must be encouraged in developing the curriculum.

Administrators should encourage instructors to provide adequately for diverse levels of student performance. A variety of activities should assist in guiding each learner to achieve optimally.

Administrators need to encourage instructors to utilise diverse evaluation procedures to ascertain student achievement. The only justification to evaluate achievement is to determine how much each student has learned. Instructors should evaluate not only subject matter learned by students, but also skills and attitudes acquired. Subject matter learned includes valuable facts, concepts, and generalisations. Appropriate skills to achieve include problem solving, creative and critical thinking, and using the library effectively. Relevant attitudes need to include appreciations for subject matter acquired in a given class, as well as a desire for life-long learning.

The Administrator and Developing Motivation

Development feelings of high morale within faculty members is needed a worthwhile goal. Faculty members possessing an adequate self-concept may exhibit a zest for doing a good job of instruction.

The administrator needs to take time to complement faculty members who prepare thoroughly for each day of quality teaching. Oral comments, as well as notes of commendation, may be presented to instructors who excel in the teaching arena. As end result may well be that instructors possess a higher energy level for the professional academic and/or vocational world in preparing objectives, learning activities, and evaluation procedures.

Administrators also have significant roles to play in each of the following endeavours to increase motivation of faculty members:

1. attempt to achieve an adequate level of salary and level of remuneration for professional services performed by faculty members. Low morale and low motivation definitely may come about if salary schedules are low in payment to professional faculty members. Inadequate reimbursement for professional teaching may require that selected faculty members obtain a second job to maintain a desired standard of living;
2. reward faculty members, orally and/or in writing, for publishing manuscripts in professional education and academic journals;
3. praise faculty members who speak in a meaningful manner to diverse civic and professional groups on educational and academic topics.

The Administrator and Problem Solving

Faculty members, as do all individuals in society, experience problems in developing and implementing the curriculum. Administrative support needs to be in evidence for instructors who truly are innovative in improving course offsprings. Innovations being tested in teaching/learning situations must:

1. guide learners to perceive purpose or reasons for learning;
2. assist students to attach meaning and understanding to subject matter being acquired;
3. facilitate in the development of positive attitudes within each learner;
4. attempt to capture student interests;

5. guide students to achieve skills in critical thinking, creative thinking, and problem solving.

Emotional support from administrators can do much to facilitate recommended curricular innovations in the educational arena. Problems that arise in developing the curriculum need to be identified and relevant solutions sought. Administrators become key individuals in lending support to faculty members in identifying and solving problems.

Additional areas which require the utilisation of problem solving methods involving administrators and faculty members include the following:

1. absenteeism and tardiness on the part of students;
2. disruptions by students in the class setting;
3. deficient test results and inadequately developed term projects by students.

Flexible steps of problem solving which may be followed by faculty members and administrators include the following:

1. identify the problem or problem areas involved in the curriculum;
2. gather information and data in attempting to solve the problem(s);
3. develop a hypothesis or answer to the identified problem;
4. test the hypothesis in actual, real-life situations.

In Conclusion

The administrator has definite roles to perform in guiding faculty members to improve the curriculum. These roles include:

1. assisting faculty members to develop purposeful objectives for students to attain;
2. supporting the utilising of a variety of learning activities for student interaction and learning. Emphasising the use of diverse valid and reliable appraisal techniques to notice learner progress;

3. **motivating faculty members to increased energy levels to engage in quality instructional procedures;**
4. **developing problem solving attitudes within faculty members.**

6

School Organisational Climate and the Administrator

There certainly are numerous classifications of environments involving administrators end other school workers. Which kind of organisational climate(s) should be available to guide optimal achievement of all involved in the school and class setting?

Morale of Faculty Members and the Administrator

Certainly, an administrator will desire to develop and maintain high morale within educators in the school/class setting. Thus, feelings of accomplishment are in evidence. Administrators and teachers believe that relevant objectives have been identified and are being attained. A quality curriculum is then in evidence. Faculty meetings, workshops and other means of inservice education truly result in a programme of education which ultimately provides for individual differences among learners. What is emphasised in inservice education is not busy work nor mundane, but significant and salient. Administrators and teachers feel intrinsic motivation due to satisfying programmes of staff development which aid students to achieve more optimally.

At the same time, inservice education programmes are not taking up an excessive amount of time. Administrators and teachers have their own personal lives to live. Self-actualisation goals need to be attained and not institutional or school purposes alone. Both personal needs and the needs of the profession must receive adequate emphasis.

An administrator emphasising criteria to develop high morale will:

1. Have input from teachers in terms of goals to be achieved in diverse inservice education programmes. Inservice education procedures must aid teachers in solving vital problems in curriculum development.
2. Assist in obtaining needed instructional materials and supplies so that teachers might truly provide for each student in the school/class setting.
3. Work for improved salaries and fringe benefits for teachers.
4. Recognise teachers for guiding learners to achieve well in ongoing lessons and units.
5. Encourage a wholesome school environment dedicated to the growth of faculty members and students.
6. Emhasise teachers living enriched personal lives with adequate opportunities to grow personally and professionally.

Social Interaction

Most individuals seemingly have feelings of wanting to belong within a social setting. Thus, administrators and teachers wish to communicate with others in an informal way. Being close to others socially is a wish and need. When problems and crises arise, the involved person has a need to communicate and be accepted by others. Being able to confide in others is valued highly. Having learners in the school/class setting achieve optimally is very fulfilling to most teachers and administrators. Thus, institutional needs are being emphasised. However, other needs are salient also, such as feelings to belonging and acceptance.

What might an administrator do to guide the self and others to have social needs met?

1. Provide an attractive lounge in which administrators and teachers may converse in an unstructured way.

2. Listen to personal problems expressed by teachers. Provide sympathetic understanding and emotional support for these problematic areas.

3. Prior to conducting workshop sessions and faculty meetings, provide refreshments for involved participants. Informal get together, such as these should aid in reducing feelings of tension and anxiety.

4. Attempt to secure an adequate number of sick day leaves for teachers to minimise feelings of anxiety over absences due to illness.

5. Praise individual teachers for effort put forth in quality teaching endeavours.

The Administrative as a Model

Teachers and other school workers need to observe a model which emphasises excellence in the curriculum. Thus, the administrator needs to be a sincere individual in putting forth effort as an educational leader. Expecting others in the school/class setting to achieve well without administrative example, may not work in the direction of developing a quality curriculum. The administrator must be a knowledgeable person in the area of developing objectives which are meaningful, purposeful, and provide for individual differences among learners.

A positive administrative model might well emphasise the following:

1. Show leadership in implementing inservice education programmes which meet the needs of the self and other school workers. Thus, relevant school problems must to identified and solved.

2. Demonstrate effective teaching procedures to involved teachers.

3. Show interest in the work of each teacher and support service worker.

4. Be polite and friendly to those involved in developing the school curriculum. Assist teachers were possible.

5. Achieve quality rapport with parents, the press, television, and radio. Report to society, achievements and accomplishments of the involved school.

What is Deemphasise

There are selected cautions for administrators to follow. The cautions pertain to emphasising the mundane and hindrances in teaching and learning. Which situations might well minimise developing relevance in the curriculum?

1. An excess number of issued bulletins for teachers to read in terms of school announcements.
2. Requests/commands for an excessive number of forms to be completed by teachers and other school workers.
3. Interfering announcements made over the intercom system which disrupt teaching-learning situations.
4. Being insensitive to the needs, interest, and purposes of school workers.
5. Emphasising achieving the goals of the school and neglecting consideration of human desires, wishes, and wants.

In Closing

Administrators need to be cognizant of developing an educational environment which enables teachers, support personnel, and students to achieve optimally. Factors which optimise and minimise human achievement need to be identified. Goals need establishing which guide in achieving organisational goals of the school as well as personal needs possessed by involved human beings.

7

Motivation and the Administrator

Which situations, environments, or factors motivate leaders in the curriculum? There are diverse theories and hypotheses which attempt to explain energy levels of administrators.

Behaviourism and Administration

Advocates of behaviourism in attempting to explain motivation believe the environment manipulates all human beings. Thus, the individual does not choose or make selections. Rather, forces external to school leaders actually motivate. Rewards in school and in society do the actual motivating.

An administrator reflecting behaviourism encourages teachers and other school workers to establish precise objectives. The sequential, measurable ends are attainable. Learners in the classroom setting with teacher guidance experience activities to achieve the desired objectives. Ultimately, the teacher measures if a learner has/has not achieved the stated ends. Successful learners in goal attainment are provided new experiences to achieve the next sequential objective. Primary (actual prizes) and secondary (tokens to be exchanged for prizes) reinforcers may be given to students for achieving at an appropriate level. Motivated students should be an important end result.

Extrinsic rewards should also be utilised to motivate teachers to do quality teaching. The administrator might then:

1. praise teachers personally for doing well in teaching;

2. give recognition as faculty meetings for outstanding endeavours by individual teachers;

3. send personal letters indicating appreciation to each teacher revealing professionalism in teaching;

4. announce in school assemblies, specific ways in which teachers individually are stimulating students to achieve optimally;

5. attempt to secure merit ratings for teachers. Thus, teachers who achieve well in teaching would receive increased pay for their efforts.

B.F. Skinner is a leading advocate of behaviourism as a psychology of learning which emphasises reinforcement as a motivator.

Management by Objective (MBO) and the Administrator

Selected educators recommend goal theory as a means of motivating administrators and other school personnel. MBO is one approach. Administrators and teachers develop scientific objectives for a school to attain. The stated ends emphasise priorities for attainment by the school. Effort is then put forth by involved individuals in the school to achieve the precisely written objectives. Motivation is inherent in perceiving clearly, developed, cooperatively arranged objectives involving administrators, teachers, and other school workers.

Careful monitoring is involved to determine if the objectives are being attained. If the precise ends are not being attained, effort needs to be put forth to achieve the desired goals. Administrators and faculty members feel encouraged when measurable ends are being attained.

An administrator emphasising a goals theory to motivate the self and others stresses:

1. teachers and other school workers having input in deciding upon worthwhile goals for a school to attain;

2. objectives written as precisely as possible. Clarity in stated intents is a motivator for involved educators to achieve;

3. establishment of priorities among accepted objectives;
4. resource (money, equipment and effort) used to achieve precise objectives;
5. monitor to determine if objectives are being achieved, as a given school year progresses;
6. corrections in means may need to be made during the ensuing school year to correct deficiencies if objectives are not being attained.

Humanism and the Administrator

An administrator emphasising humanism as a school psychology, realises that human as well as institutional needs must be met. To achieve school goals is not adequate. Each school worker has personal needs which must, if at all possible, also be fulfilled. Achieving self actualisation is a key goal to emphasise, humanities advocate. The late A.H. Maslow stressed the following needs be met by individuals, in general ascending order of complexity so that self-actualisation may be a relevant end result.

1. *Psychological needs.* Adequate food, clothing, and shelter should be available to all individuals.
2. *Security needs.* Each person needs to possess feelings of safety. Threatening situations for administrators, teachers, other school workers, and students do not make for feelings of security.
3. *Belonging needs.* Persons individually need to be accepted by others in a group setting. Individuals who are isolates or on fringe areas of being accepted cannot possess feelings of belonging.
4. *Esteem needs.* Each human being desires to have prestige within a group setting. Thus, an individual is known for positive accomplishments in one or more areas. A person being known as one who has not/cannot achieve is not to likely to be recognised for accomplishment endeavours.

5. *Self-actualisation needs.* Administrators having attained self-actualisation have, in degrees, achieved becoming the kind of person desired. Thus, gaps are minimised in terms of wishing a certain ideal and the actual personal achievement of that goal.

Administrators emphasising need fulfilment attempt to determine his/her own wants, as well as those of school workers. Definite attempts are made to fulfil the identified needs. Humanism as a psychology of motivation is then in evidence. The humanist administrator realises that lower level needs, such as physiological and safety, must be met before more complex needs (belonging, esteem, and self-actualisation are emphasised).

Ultimately, the goals of the school system can be attained more adequately if personal needs of individuals have been met.

Expectancy Theory and the Administrator

How do feelings to expectancy motivate administrators and other school workers? Three dimensions need elaboration in expectancy theory.

The first concept *valence* emphasises attractions that an administrator might receive from his/her professional position. Feelings of prestige, job satisfaction and adequate income may well attract administrators to their professional roles. Certainly, a lack of the above named feelings might well encourage an administrator to seek self-fulfilment in another job, occupation, or vocation. Valences, then emphasises that which attracts an administrator, or any individual to a specific situation.

The second concept *instrumentality* emphasises the probability that a given valence will occur, as perceived by the perceiver. What then are the odds/probability in job satisfaction to occur? The higher the likelihood that a valence (or valences) will occur, the more likely that individuals, administrators, included, will develop feelings of motivation. A lack of motivation occurs when one or several significant valences do not accrue. Rewards must be forthcoming for the involved administrator to believe in instrumentality, or success in achieving one or more valences.

The third concept *expectancy* emphasises beliefs pertaining to effort put forth in achieving goals. Does hard on the part of the administrator make for success in leadership roles? Or, are too many chance factors in life involved whereby effort put forth in administration makes little or no difference in attempted objectives achieved? Expectancy as a concept implies that engaged effort will pay off in goal attainment. Thus, effort put forth is an intrinsic motivator.

Victor Vroom was an originator of the valance-instrumentality-expectancy (VIE) theory of motivation.

In Conclusion

There are diverse psychologies providing models in motivation for administrators and other school workers.

1. Behaviourism emphasises positive reinforcement. Rewards may then be utilised to reinforce (strengthen) desired behaviour.
2. Management by Objective (MBO) stresses the significance of precise, clearly stated objectives developed by administrators and school workers in general. Once, measurable objectives have been developed and accepted, human beings are clear in terms of roles and expectations. Motivation increases with clarity of intent and purpose.
3. Humanism places strong emphasis upon meeting needs of administrators and faculty. Each person is motivated in achieving self-actualisation. Physiological and safety needs must be met prior to attaining higher order needs such as belonging, esteem, and self-actualisation.
4. Expectancy theory emphasises the importance that beliefs have in motivating human behaviour. Thus, valence, instrumentality, and expectancy become salient concepts in motivating human behaviour.

Administrators need to study, analyse, and ultimately develop, viable, defensible theories of motivation. To achieve optimally, individuals need to be motivated. Goals of the school and curriculum might then be achievable more comprehensively than would be true of non-motivated individuals.

8

Preparing Quality School Administrators

Quality administrators are needed in the public schools. Each administrator needs to guide and facilitate teachers to provide the best curriculum possible for each student. Persons have worth and value. Individuals need to achieve optimally in each curriculum area.

The Psychology of Learning and the School Administrator

Administrators of public schools need to possess comprehensive knowledge in educational psychology and how it affects the learning process. Thus, each school administrator needs to understand behaviourism and reinforcement theory. The use of behaviourally stated objectives, criterion reference tests (CRT), mastery learning, and state mandated testing, as concepts, need to be mastered by principals and supervisors. Also, methods of encouraging student achievement through extrinsic rewards need to be understood and implemented. Primary and secondary reinforcers can be used as extrinsic motivation. These learnings need emphasis in preservice preparation of principals and superintendents.

Administrators also need to understand the tenets of humanism, as a psychology of learning. School administrators then need to attach meaning to tenets of self-actualisation of students. Needs of students must be met by the school and home setting. In developing the curriculum, students with teacher guidance need to select objectives, learning opportunities, and appraisal procedures. Student choice in definitely involved in selecting *what* to learn scope and *when* (sequence) the subject matter is to be acquired. The affective (feeling) dimension is highly significant to develop within.students.

The writer also believes that school administrators need to understand and be able to utilise Robert Gagne's task analysis procedures. If a student in the public school is not achieving adequately, Gagne's task analysis is an excellent model to utilise in assisting optimal student progress. The last three levels—developing concepts, attaining rules, and problem solving—in particular, are highly significant.

Lastly, educational administrators need to attach meaning to a strategy emphasising order in learning opportunities provided students. Jerome Bruner's model is excellent. Manipulative materials (concrete) need to be used first in teaching. In sequence, iconic (semi-concrete) means are to be utilised in teaching, followed by symbolic (abstract) activities and experiences.

The Philosophy of Education and the Administrator

Administrators need to possess a thorough knowledge of philosophy in developing a rationale for selecting objectives, learning opportunities, and appraisal procedures. Thus, a principal of superintendent needs adequate knowledge of experimentalism as a philosophy of education. Experimentalists believe that change is reality in life. One can only know what is experienced. With change and experiences, problems arise. Identified problems need solutions. The solutions are tentative and not absolutes. School and society need to be integrated and not isolated entities. Experimentalists administrators need to be highly proficient in the problem solving arena.

Administrators emphasising realism as a philosophy of education believe that reality as it truly is can be known in whole or in part. Whatever exists then can be known wholly or partially and is measurable. Objective reality is knowable and can be measured precisely. Mathematics and science, in particular, contain precise, measurable subject matter. Other curriculum areas, in degrees, also contain specific, observable content.

Principals and superintendents believing in realism stress the utilisation of measurably stated objectives and criterion referenced testing (CRT) in the school curriculum.

In the area of administration of schools, principals and superintendents as realists advocate the use of management by objectives (MBO) in operating the total school. Or, to be cost effective, the concepts of programme, planning, budgeting system (PPBS) are emphasised by realist administrators. To determine if the school system is on track for achieving objectives in MBO or PPBS, programme evaluation review technique (PERT) is emphasised. A realist administrator then believes that progress in learning by students is measurable and observable. Achievement of objectives of the school can also be measured, such as in MBO and PPBS.

Principals and superintendents adhering to idealism as a philosophy of education believe in an idea centred curriculum. Students then need to experience a subject matter, not activity centred curriculum. In each academic area, learners need to attain relevant facts, concepts, and generalisations. Generalisations or universals, in particular, are significant for student attainment. Textbooks, workbooks, and worksheets, especially and carefully selected by teachers and administrators, assist students to acquire vital subject matter.

Students need to achieve common, essential learnings in subject matter. The basics need to be carefully chosen by teachers and administrators so that each student might attain worthwhile, vital subject matter. Ideas that are enduring and stable need to be achieved by learners.

An idealist administrator then believes in general education for all students. The curriculum of idealism must be non-convocational. Vocational education can come later, after a quality general education is received by all students. These principals and superintendents are quite academically inclined in terms of emphasising what students should learn.

An existentialist principal or superintendent emphasises that each person develop personal commitments in life. The existentialist individually choose and makes decisions. There are no absolutes or universals. Thus, no essence or goals are given to persons. Rather, an individual is born and then must select his/her own goals in a completely open ended environment. An existentialist administrator believes that the environment and life itself is ridiculous and absurd. Within this ridiculous and absurd environment, decisions need to be made by the involved individual. Others cannot be blamed for the consequences of a personal decision made.

The principal or superintendent advocating existentialism as a philosophy of education encourages teachers to also make decisions and assume responsibilities for choices made. Blame cannot be placed on others for results of a decision or choice made.

In addition to understanding and being able to implement experimentalism, realism, idealism, and existentialism as appropriate philosophies for school administrators, the principal of superintendent should also understand specific philosophies to utilise in the classroom. The writer would recommend that future administrators understand:

1. essentialism or the basics in the curriculum;
2. activity centred methods of teaching, such as the utilisation of learning centres;
3. project methods of teaching;
4. contractual means of instruction;
5. accountability approaches for teachers;
6. pupil-teacher planning in the classroom.

The Psychology of Learning and the Student

Administrators need to have a thorough understanding of diverse schools of thought in the psychology of learning.

One school of thought emphasises behaviourism. Behaviourism emphasises the use of measurably stated objectives. The behaviourally stated objectives may be arranged in ascending order of complexity. After instruction, it can be measured if a student has/has not achieved sequential objectives.

Diverse states have mandated testing for students to notice their progress in learning. The lay public seemingly wants measurable results to notice student progress. If the state mandated tests are directly related to the objectives of instruction, behaviourism is certainly in evidence. Mastery learning, Instructional Management Systems (IMS), Individually Prescribed Instruction (IPI), and management by objective (MBO) emphasise behaviourism as a psychology of learning. A logical curriculum is then in evidence.

Principals and superintendents need to be well versed in humanism, as a psychology of learning. Humanism advocates concepts such as pupil-teacher planning, learners achieving self-actualisation, input from students in developing the curriculum, decision-making by learners, as well as student seeking and pacing goals, learning opportunities, and appraisal procedures. The teacher in humanistic psychology procedures is a stimulator and a guide in the learning arena for students. The student needs to be rather heavily involved in selecting goals, learning opportunities, and appraisal procedures with teacher guidance. A psychological curriculum is then in evidence.

Child growth and development characteristics need adequate emphasis in course work for school administrators. Jean Piaget's stages of child development then need emphasis in educational psychology as well as implementation in the classroom. Thus, the sensorimotor, preoperational, concrete operations, and formal operations stages are significant in the educational psychology arena to prepare principals and superintendents for their roles in the school setting.

To further emphasis sequence in learning, the prospective school administrator needs to understand a reputable model. Jerome Bruner stresses the use of enactive (manipulative), iconic (semi-concrete), and symbol (abstract materials), in that sequence of order for each lesson taught to students.

Sociology and Anthropology for Administrators

Students in the school setting come from diverse socio-economic levels. These socio-economic levels have tremendous implications for teaching students. There are diverse norms and roles played by individuals in society. Sanctions are applied in society to uphold these norms as well as roles. A changing family is definitely in evidence in society. Students that come from unstable home situations need certain kinds of assistance. The writer believes strongly that principals and superintendents need to understand educational sociology and its implications for curriculum development and the teaching of students.

Anthropology and its study is highly significant in the preparation of school administrators. Each culture and subculture has its very own beliefs, values and traditions. Too frequently, feelings of ethnocentrism abound. Respect for other cultures definitely needs to be in evidence. Thus, principals and superintendents need to understand and appreciate how cultures differ from each other in art, music, architecture, customs, sports endeavours, religious beliefs, foods, eaten, and means of greeting each other.

Teaching Skills and the Curriculum

An abundance of research and content is available in guiding teachers to utilise effective teaching skills. Benjamin Bloom's taxonomy in the cognitive domain may provide prospective administrators with a wealth of information on guiding teachers and students to achieve effectively in school. Thus, in preparation programmes for school administrators, ample time needs to be in emphasis in stressing teaching skills involving:

1. the knowledge or recall level;
2. comprehension of content;
3. application of what has been learned previously;
4. analyzation of subject matter to separate into component parts;
5. synthesization of content;
6. evaluation in terms of definite criteria or standards.

Principals and superintendents also need to understand and be able to utilise concepts such as:

1. depth teaching;
2. induction and deduction;
3. scope and sequence;
4. the basics in the curriculum;
5. student input in ongoing lessons and units;
6. aims, goals, and objectives;
7. multi-media approaches;
8. evaluation of student progress;
9. organisation of the curriculum;
10. management of the classroom.

The planned curriculum (curriculum guides) needs to be understood and used in the classroom settings. The dynamic curriculum (resource units and teaching units) must be emphasised in terms of actual classroom teaching and learning situations.

To stress task analysis in the curriculum, school administrators need to attach meaning to Robert Gagne's hierarchy of objectives. The principal or superintendent then needs to understand:

1. signal learning;
2. stimulus-response;
3. motor chaining;
4. verbal chaining;
5. discriminative learnings;
6. concept development;
7. rule learning;
8. problem solving.

If a student cannot solve a problem (number 8 above), the teacher needs to assist the students to understand the rule (generalisation). If the rule has little or no meaning to the student, the involved concepts need to be taught. The teacher may go back to earlier sequential learnings, if necessary, to guide students to attain prerequisites. Gagne's hierarchy of objectives is an excellent model in task analysis for teachers and administrators to follow.

History of the Curriculum

The writer believes strongly that professional school administrators need to understand the history of education. A few key concepts and generalisations will be presented.

Puritans came to the New World in 1630 and developed a rather comprehensive system of schools for their day. The Massachusetts Law of 1642 emphasised that Puritan children should learn the principles of religion and the capital laws of their land. There was little enforcement of the Massachusetts Law of 1642. In 1647, another Massachusetts Law was passed in which each village having fifty households, by law, needed to hire an elementary school teacher or pay the assessed fine. If 100 householders were in a village, a secondary or Latin Grammar School teacher must be employed. The fines were low and some villages paid the fine rather than hiring a teacher.

The Dame School was a somewhat common elementary school in the days of the Puritans. A woman then, knowing the rudiments of reading would teach pupils one-half day to take care of household responsibilities the other half of the day. Few records were kept to emphasise any sequential learning of students. The horn-book, the Psalter, the Bible, the Westminster catechism, and the New England Primer were materials utilised to achieve religious goals. Physical punishment was a common means of disciplining pupils.

Joseph Lancaster and the Lancastrian Monitorial System of Instruction was brought to the United States in 1805. Lancaster established sequential levels of instruction in reading and arithmetic. Spelling and handwriting were correlated with reading. Individual differences were provided for with a single pupil being permitted to move on to the next class level when the material of the previous level had been mastered. Inexpensive teaching was emphasised with charts used for teaching instead of textbooks, as well as slate and sand utilised instead of pencil and paper. Methods of embarrassment, not physical punishment was utilised to discipline pupils.

Principals and superintendents need to understand the quality contributions of Johann Pestalozzi, Johann Herbart, and Friedrich Froebel. Pestalozzi's object lessons and the use of concrete materials is significant in education. Herbert's steps of teaching to teach sequence within a lesson should be meaningful to school administrators. His steps of preparation, presentation, association, generalisation, and use can still be applicable in teaching today. Froebel's emphasis upon creativity as the major goal of teaching is vital in today's classrooms.

With a study of the history of education, school administrators may notice how objectives, learning activities, and evaluation procedures have changed. Also, what has remained stable in teaching and learning also needs to be noticed. The contributions of J.M. Rice, Horace Mann, John Dewey, E.L. Thorndike, James Conant, the Progressive Education Association, and the Seven Cardinal Principles of Education need to be understood and valued by principals and superintendents.

An appreciation for change and for the contributions of significant educators and movements in education need to be understood by school administrators. Present developments in education are sequentially related to the past.

Measurement of Achievement and Research in Education

Principals and superintendents need to understand relevant concepts in the field of measurement and research. These include:

1. construct, predictive, content, and criterion validity;
2. split half, test-retest, and equivalent forms of reliability;
3. quartile deviation and standard deviation;
4. mode, mean, and median;

5. norm referenced and criterion referenced testing;
6. diverse techniques to appraise student progress. These include teacher developed appraisal procedures, as well as standardised tests;
7. experimental and control group in research;
8. experimental, correlational, survey, and historical research;
9. tests of significance (T tests and F tests);
10. research tools in using the library and the computer.

A competent administrator of schools needs to develop proficiency to measure student achievement well in an era of accountability. Also, principals and superintendents need to conduct research to improve the school curriculum. The curriculum needs rather continuous modification to assist each learner to attain optimally.

Developing Administrative Skills

The heart of the degree programme and inservice education for school administrators is in the acquisition of understanding, skills and attitudes to become quality, effective administrators.

Principals and superintendents need to develop leadership skills in diverse means of inservice education for teachers, support personnel, and supervisors. The workshop approach needs to be understood in developing large group sessions, committee endeavours, and individual study. Also, the faculty meeting concept needs to emphasise agendas and vital problems for participants to consider in assisting each student to achieve optimally. Further means of inservice education include visiting innovative schools, engaging in school research, reading and summarising content in an area of educational concern, attending professional meetings in teacher education, as well as taking course work on college and university campuses to improve the school curriculum.

School administrators need to develop feelings of high morale on the part of teachers and other school personnel. Principals and superintendents then must develop an atmosphere of respect and acceptance toward others in the school setting. A major weakness of numerous school administrators is their lack of abilities in working with selected teachers, secretaries and guidance counselors, among other school personnel. Prior to being employed in a school, principals and superintendents need to demonstrate proficiency in working with a wide variety of personalities. Having an inner circle of associates only, is not adequate. Others feel left out of decision-making if this situation exists. Morale goes downhill among faculty members if the school administrator can relate effectively to two or three teachers only.

School administrators need to be able to reward teachers and other workers in the school setting when quality performance is in evidence. Selected principals and superintendents feel very uneasy in praising anyone for tasks well done. Preservice and inservice programmes in school administration should emphasis reinforcement theory in courses taken and field work experienced.

A major responsibility of principals and superintendents is to identify and solve problems. Too frequently, school administrators hide in their offices and remain aloof from where the action to taking place. Schools of education on university campuses need to stress the importance of principals and superintendents being directly involved to provide the best possible curriculum for each learner. Teachers and other school personnel need to know that school administrators are available to provide needed positive assistance.

A quality honest public relations programme is necessary for any school. School administrators must realise that the best public relations possible for any school or school system is to guide students to achieve optimally in all facets of development. Parents and the lay public need to feel that the school setting is a highly valuable asset to their son or daughter. Principals and superintendents should communicate to parents and the lay public what classrooms are accomplishing in the field of education. Newspaper reports, radio broadcasts, television items, classroom newspapers, and school newspapers can aid in assisting the local community to understand the goals and objectives of the school. School administrators, prior to being employed, should demonstrate competency in preservice education programmes that quality public relations programmes are important for the school system as well as for parents and the lay public.

Principals and superintendents must do the best possible to get to know parents and other persons in society on a personal basis. They also need to be acquainted with students. Remaining aloof from learners and adults in society does not make for an effective administrator.

Concepts in course taken in school administration on university campus should include the following:

1. Staffing to improve learning. The best staff should be hired to teach students. Each staff member should be qualified in the area he/she is teaching. Present faculty members need to experience inservice programmes which release optimal talents possessed by teachers.
2. Business management of the school. Accurate accountability of all funds spent in a school needs to be available. The community must have confidence that school funds are spent to educate and provide the best possible curriculum for each student.
3. Management of school facilities. Classrooms and the school building should be clean, safe, and comfortable for students, teachers, and all other employees of the school district.

In Closing

. The knowledge explosion in society has changed the role(s) of the principal and superintendent. The use of software and computers alone, has made for tremendous changes in the school curriculum as well as the educational environment. The administrator of the future needs to possess much information and skills, as well as positive attitudes to function well within the framework of school and society. A comprehensive programme of preservice and inservice education is necessary to develop truly professional principals and superintendents.

9

School Administration as Decision-Making

Principals and superintendents experience numerous problems each day requiring solutions. A school administrator then needs to become a decision-maker. Shying away from difficulties generally makes for increasingly complex problems. Preservice and inservice programmes of education must stress problem solving procedures for principals and superintendents. Which problems then need identification and viable solutions in the school setting?

Hiring School Personnel

Quality individuals need to be employed in the school setting. Teachers, as one set of employees, must be carefully chosen. Students in school are valuable and possess much worth. Each teacher must provide for individual differences. Learners need to grow optimally in intellectual, social, emotional, and physical facets of growth. The classroom teacher is one who must select worthwhile objectives for student attainment. He/she needs to select learning opportunities which are interesting, purposeful, as well as meaningful. Appraisal procedures must be selected which evaluate learner achievement of stated objectives. A variety of assessment procedures must be utilised by the teacher to appraise all facets of a student's development.

Teachers need to emphasise balance among objectives such as emphasising understandings, skills, and attitudinal goals. Rational balance needs to be in evidence among these three kinds of goals.

In providing for fast, average, and slow achievers, a multi-media approach in teaching should be in evidence. Students do possess diverse learning styles. Thus, audio-visual aids, reading materials, and excursions should be in the offing to assist learners to achieve optimally.

How might new teachers to be selected who can implement desired philosophies and psychologies of teaching?

1. see experienced teachers in action prior to their being employed in the receiving school;
2. observe beginning teachers in their student teaching experiences an university students;
3. have new experienced and beginning teachers demonstrate teaching skills, prior to their being hired in the receiving school;
4. discuss with prospective teachers recommended procedures in teaching. Take careful note of knowledge and attitudes displayed to the profession of teaching;
5. let these teachers take a position on issues in education, such as an activity centred versus a subject centred curriculum;
6. have employed teachers in the school visit with and discuss trends in teaching with the prospective teacher(s). Secure feedback from these employed teachers on their impressions of the interviewee;
7. call individuals by phone who wrote recommendations for the prospective teacher to be employed. Ask specific questions about selected traits of the prospective teacher.

Ultimately, a synthesis needs to be made pertaining to which teacher will be hired to fill the vacancy.

Working with Teachers in the School Setting

School administrators must be able to work effectively with others in the school. A polished person is not really desired. Rather, an honest individual who can provide leadership to release the creative abilities of all teachers is needed. Too frequently, principals and superintendents are able to work well with two or three inner circle persons only. This is indeed unfortunate. Rather, a school administrator, such as a building principal, should be able to motivate *all* teachers. If the inner circle concept exists, too many will feel left out of decision-making activities. The self concept of the isolated teachers goes downhill. Rather, the principal must communicate and work effectively with each teacher as a person having much worth.

Respect for others is a philosophy of life and must be learned. An effective person is able to work with diverse kinds of personalities, not the polished and influential person only. The writer would like to recommend the following to help school administrators to work more harmoniously with other human beings:

1. study philosophy to learn diverse schools of thought involving experimentalism, realism, idealism, and experimentalism. Pre-service and inservice programmes of education for principals and superintendents should have as a major educational outcome—respect for other persons;
2. learn about diverse cultures in society and avoid feelings of ethnocentrism. Cultures different from each other in music, art, religious, beliefs, customs, language, and beliefs;
3. evaluate the self in terms of being accepting of others. If hostile feelings exist or shunning of others is in evidence, attempt to locate relevant causes or reasons;
4. take course work on a university campus on public relations in education. Attempt to relate the content to actual use in the local school setting. Evaluate the instructor of the course in terms of criteria for quality pubic relations. When does or does not the instructor follow desirable standards in public relations?
5. work hard on achieving the goal or respecting others. Effort can go a long way;

6. do not force your beliefs in education on others. A school administrator can become too ambitious in working for quick changes. His/her ideas may or may not have merit. Each consideration must be evaluated in terms of desirable standards;
7. take a test on being rigid in thinking, such as the *Rokeach Test of Dogmatism*. Use the results to become flexible and open in one's thinking.

Working with the Lay Public

School administrators need to develop proficiency in working effectively with parents and others in the societal arena. Too frequently, principals and superintendents have depended upon "putting the best foot forward", rather than substance. It then mattered more *how* something was said as compared to *what* was communicated. Polish, physical beauty, and methods are significant to the communicator to the degree that effective communication, honestly presented is in evidence. Honesty is defined as harmonising with truly happens in a school or school system with that which is communicated. Too frequently, a lack of congruency exists between with transpires or happens and what is actually communicated to the lay public.

The effective school administrator desires to communicate regularly with the lay public. A broad knowledge base of the school or school system together with visions or ideals can make for quality reporting to the constituency. Principals and superintendents need goals which represent standards to aim toward. A school administrator who merely manipulates people to stay in power or keep his/her job has lost ideals and dreams. No doubt, many principals and superintendents who lack goals focus so much on the struggle for existence and the survival of the fittest, to the degree that aims and purposes of education are lost. Professional responsibilities are then relinquished and unethical behaviour is an end result.

To remedy deficiencies in the roles of many school administrators, the following are pertinent in that school administrators:

1. need to focus on vital goals of education and the processes of implementing these ends;
2. must zero is on assisting each student to achieve optimally in the public schools;
3. should have relevant standards to communicate to the lay public in terms of using the media of radio, television, newspapers, open house, and oral language in one to one contact with individuals;
4. need to be effective speakers at civic and professional meetings to communicate progress as well as needs of a school. The content, not the medium, is always the message. Accuracy of ideas needs to be expressed. The ideas represent reality as it truly is, in the school setting.

Improving the Curriculum

The school setting should offer the best curriculum possible for each student. Each learner needs to achieve as much as possible in each curriculum area. Classes need to be offered which meet subject matter, skills, and attitudinal needs of students. Politics need to be left out completely in developing the curriculum. Rather, a scientific study should be made pertaining to objectives students need to achieve. Which understandings, abilities, and attitudes are deemed necessary for student attainment? The student, as well as parents and the lay public, perceive needs in education differently. How can all these diverse perceptions be harmonised? What should be the role of each state in mandating requirements? The school administrator has a leading role in providing leadership in curriculum development. A principal or superintendent must not reveal ignorance or be uninformed about vital concepts and generalisations in education. Recently, an administrator in a faculty meeting revealed he did not believe that concepts such as the separate subjects, correlated, fused, or integrated curricula existed. He even accused the faculty member who mentioned these concepts in the meeting of making up ideas to substantiate biased beliefs. In other words, the school administrator here was ill informed about vital ideas in education. It behooves principals and superintendents to be extremely well informed in educational studies and content. An administrator should not depend upon polish, manipulation, slickness, and coercion to attain his/her goals in education and in life.

What should principals and superintendents do to assist in improving the curriculum for each student?

1. they need to be highly knowledgeable about current trends in each curriculum area. Administrators need to do much reading from current periodicals and other literature dealing with recent writings in education;
2. subject matter acquired from reading content on education should be discussed with teachers in an open ended, not dogmatic approach;
3. principals and superintendents should attend professional conventions and meetings on improving the curriculum. Strict attention needs to be paid to ideas expressed by speakers on how to provide for individual differences in the classroom;
4. administrators should visit innovative classrooms inside and outside the local school system to become knowledgeable about current trends in education;
5. administrators should discuss with other principals and superintendents on how to assist slow, average, and fast students achieve optimally;
6. they need to work harmoniously with the faculty to improve the curriculum;
7. administrators need to secure input from parents and the lay public on ways of improving teaching-learning situations;
8. principals and superintendents should work in the direction of balancing state mandations with local needs of students in the school-community setting.

Administrators and the School Secretary

The secretary or secretaries of a school may well be the first point of contact for parents and the lay public, students, teachers, and other school personnel. Each secretary needs to show traits of politeness, acceptance, and assistance to others. Too frequently, a secretary is considerate of the school administrator only. The secretary may almost be a dual personality in being kind and helpful to the principal or superintendent and extremely rude to others.

Sometimes, secretaries secure their positions due to influence from others in society. The school secretary was not hired based or merit, but rather on being the wife or friend of influential people in society. The school then is struck with the mess. No amount of talk by the school administrator to the secretary modifies the behaviour of the latter. The rudeness and inconsiderateness of the secretary in enduring. She reveals that it is not necessary to be accepting of others and doing satisfactory work.

What can a school administrator do to ensure optimal achievement from secretaries?

1. inservice education programmes are a must for school secretaries. Roles and role expectations of each secretary need to be clarified;
2. each secretary needs to be evaluated periodically in terms of quality criteria. Feedback of results to the involved secretary is important;
3. interview carefully new secretaries for employment. Let secretaries know what will be expected of them;
4. show appreciation and respect for quality work performed by the school secretary;
5. provide certificates of achievement based on quality work performed and not on the number of years entrenched within the system;
6. secretaries need to realise they serve a larger population, as compared to office personal only.

In Conclusion

Numerous highly significant decisions need to be made by the school administrator. The decisions include:

1. hiring quality school personnel;
2. working effectively with teachers;
3. interacting positively with the lay public;
4. improving the school curriculum;
5. developing proficient secretaries in the school setting.

10

School Administration and the Psychology of Learning

Each principal, supervisor, or superintendent utilises selected criteria from the educational psychology arena which guide in making choices and decisions in the school-class setting. Thus, administrators need to study, analyse and ultimately implement a desired synthesis of content from the psychology of learning.

Humanism and the School Administrator

Humanism as a psychology of learning emphasises selected tenets in teaching-learning situations. Among other generalisations, humanism advocates:

1. Pupils having ample opportunities to choose what to learn (objectives) as well as the means of learning (activities and experiences).
2. Mutual trust being emphasised between among teachers, administrators, and pupils.
3. Humaneness being stressed in the school-class setting with pupils selecting and pacing their own learning within a flexible environment.
4. Wholeness of the learner receiving primary emphasis in teaching-learning situations. Thus, the intellectual, physical, social and emotional person in his/her entirety must be recognised. The feeling dimensions of each individual, especially is to be prized highly.

5. The authentic individual being valued highly as compared to facades to hide the true human being.

The humanist administrator may well emphasise criteria such as the following, in working with others in the school-class setting:

1. Teachers being authentic individuals in selecting open ended objectives and learning activities in the school curriculum and the curriculum of life.
2. Relationship between administrators and school personnel being open, honest, and filled with trust. Being afraid of expressing desired opinions and ideas in the school-class setting would be opposite of the thinking of humanists.
3. Needs being met of each individual in the school environment. A.H. Maslow, humanist psychologist, provided an excellent model which may be followed in meeting human needs. Thus, for example, school administrators would be concerned about meeting physiological needs of each individual (adequate nutritious food, sleep, clothing and shelter), security needs, belonging needs, esteem needs, and self actualisation needs. The humanist school administrator realises that workers in the school-class setting can do well only if the previously named needs are met, in the order presented generally. Among other physiological needs, proper diet and rest would need fulfilment by each person before other needs become relevant, such as security needs. Feelings of insecurity make for a lack of achievement on the part of individuals and must be remedied before belonging needs can be met.
4. The feelings (affective or attitudinal dimension) of each person being given utmost attention in the school arena.

Thus, for example, teachers and administrators should feel free to express personal values and beliefs in an atmosphere of respect. The authentic person realises that feelings of individuals are an important consideration when describing and appraising human behaviour. Human beings are valuing and prizing individuals; knowledge and skills then are subjective and not objective to the involved individual.

Behaviourism and the School Administrator

Behaviourism, among other generalisations, emphasises the following tenets:

1. Teachers determining measurable objective are related learning activities to attain these desired ends for pupils.
2. Programmed learning being emphasised in teaching-learning situations. Thus, pupils may progress on their own unique levels of achievement in small, sequential steps of learning. Learners are basically successful in achieving content in each of these ordered series of items.
3. Teachers reinforcing learnings obtained by pupils. These reinforces may pertain to the use of verbal and nonverbal praise. Or, physical prizes may also be utilised to reward desirable behaviour.

School administrators emphasising the significance of behaviourism tend to believe in the following:

1. Accountability movements to determine teacher proficiency in teaching. Thus, with the utilisation of measurable objectives, teacher effectiveness in teaching can be determined in terms of pupils having achieved these stated ends after instruction.
2. Management by objectives (MBO) and/or PPBS (Programme, Planning, Budget, System). Administrative performance may then be measured against predetermined measurable objectives.
3. Rewarding teachers for doing a good job of teaching. The school administrator adhering to behaviourism may utilise much verbal praise to shape teacher behaviour in a desirable way within the framework

of teaching-learning situations. He/she may also work in the direction of obtaining merit pay salaries rather than a salary schedule based on the number of years a person has taught and the level of education obtained.

Gastalt Psychology and the School Administrator

Gestaltists emphasise the significance of the whole or entire person being involved in learning. Thus, the intellectual, social, emotional and physical facets of a person are involved in any given experience. One then does not enter an activity intellectually only, but with wholeness instead. Problem solving activities are vital for pupils. Pupils with teacher guidance may then identify relevant problems and seek possible solutions. Insight may be a highly relevant method of obtaining possible solutions to vital problems. Previous experiences are rearranged and reordered to obtain insight. Problematic situations occur when individuals face a state of disequilibrium. To be in a state of disequilbrium human beings face a problem, several problems, or a dilemma situation. After adequate solutions to problems have occurred, the person moved back to a state of equilibrium.

Implications for school administrators adhering to the Gastalt school of psychology in the school setting may well be the following:

1. Teachers, other social workers, and pupils are wholistic. Physical, social, and emotional needs of human beings must be met in addition to intellectual development.
2. Problem solving activities for pupils need to be emphasised in the school curriculum. These problems should be realistic and life-like.
3. Teachers, principals, and supervisors need to identify and solve problems in the school-class setting. Administrators alone should not identify and offer solutions to problematic situations. The wholeness concept is then lacking in the educational arena.

> Everyone in the school environment cooperatively should be involved in identifying and solving problems when decisions affect the involved individual.

In Summary

Administrators need to study diverse theories of school administration. Each theory has its pros and cons. Ultimately, the administrator needs to select those principles of administering the school which assist in developing optimal teacher and student achievement.

11

School Administration and the Curriculum

The role of the administrator in the school curriculum has not been clearly defined. Numerous manuscripts published in professional journals, as well as textbooks in school administration, have attempted to pinpoint definite roles that an administrator should perform. However, there is a lack of agreement as to what these roles are or should be.

Roles of the Administrator in the School Setting

The school administrator should provide leadership in guiding teachers in the selection of goals for students to attain. The goals may be open-ended or general in nature. The goals can also be precise and specific. Thus, learner achievement may be measured against the measurably objectives.

The administrator needs to be knowledgeable about objectives in different curriculum areas in order to provide quality leadership. Opposite would be where the blind lead the blind in not knowing which objectives to stress in teaching-learning situations.

Goals and objectives selected should:

1. be relevant for students to achieve;
2. provide for diverse capacity and achievement levels of learners;
3. stimulate interest in learning;

4. guide in establishing purpose or reasons for participating in ongoing activities and experience.

The above named criteria provide broad guidelines in developing the curriculum. Even for general objectives, the goals need to be stated in a manner which provide direction in terms of which understandings, skills, and attitudes will be stressed. Thus, the following are general goals but they do indicate *what* will be taught.

To develop within the pupil:

1. an understanding that each paragraph needs to possess coherence of ideas,
2. skill to read content critically in separating facts from opinions, accurate statements from inaccurate content, as well as factual knowledge versus fantasy;
3. an attitude of wanting to learn more about the unit presently being emphasised in the curriculum.

Each of the above general objectives does give guidance to the teacher in emphasising *what* will be taught, such as in general objective number one-pupils after teaching has occurred will attach meaning to *coherence* of ideas in a paragraph, as distinguished from other kinds or types of learning.

A school or school system may wish to emphasise specific objectives in ongoing units of study. Thus, after instruction, it can be determined if students have or have not achieved an objective. The following emphasise precise, measurable ends:

1. Given an editorial, the student will read the content and list two facts and two opinions.
2. Given a set of scrambled sentences, the students will arrange the sentences so that proper *sequence* is in evidence.

The administrator then has an important responsibility in providing leadership to improve the quality of objectives in the school curriculum.

Administrative guidance is also needed in emphasising *process* goals when working in the area of curriculum improvement. For any committee to function well and come up with the best end results possible, teachers and the administrator need to:

1. stay on the topic being pursued. Disgressing from the topic wastes time and energy. Teacher's and administrator's time is valuable;
2. seek input from all individual. If selected participants do not contribute within the committee, the end product then does not represent the thinking of all members. There are administrators who are very weak indeed in securing participation of all participants in a committee;
3. respect ideas from all participants. If content presented by a committee member is not respected, the involved person generally will refrain from participation in committee endeavours. Too frequently, the game of politics is played by administrators in determining whose ideas will/will not be respected;
4. clarify ideas presented. A committee must be certain that ideas presented are understood clearly. Ambiguous concepts and vague generalisations must be avoided by committee members.

It is difficult to be a quality leader in guiding discussions within a group setting. A polished leader having no other guidelines to present in committee work hardly will suffice. The 'smooth television personality' with few other assets is not able to provide leadership in improving the curriculum.

A second task for administrators is to stimulate teachers to select learning activities in guiding students to achieve worthwhile objectives. The chosen activities must provide for diverse learning styles of individual pupils. Each student has much worth and needs to achieve in an optimal manner. The focal point of public schools is to assist pupils to learn as much as individual capabilities permit. Public schools do not exist to have administrators receive high salaries or prestige. Rather, students need to achieve in order that they may become creative beings attaining self-realisation.

Frequently, terms such as the following are thrown around by national study groups advocating change and reform in education:

1. *Time on task.* It almost sounds as if the students are like a machine in that pupils are able to study continuously and not emphasise human traits. The time on task beliefs state that students learn more if they keep studying and achieve desired objectives. "Time on task" really does not say anything worthwhile. Common knowledge is involved in stating that a student achieves more, if he/she stays on the topic being pursued. A more worthwhile facet of the phenomena time on task would be in finding out *how* teachers can improve student's involvement pertaining to the subject matter being learned.

   A student, however, is not a machine in being able to absorb more and more content from diverse academic areas. Rather, the pupil is a human being with feelings, needs, wants, and attitudes. Thus, the affective dimension of the student needs to be fulfilled. The learner experiences feelings of fatigue, joy, contentment, as well as disappointment.

2. *Basic skills.* Too frequently in newsreports, the concept *basic skills* is mentioned and elaborated upon. It is stated generally that skills can be identified which all students need to master. These are basic or essential skills. First of all, it probably is impossible to select skills that *all* pupils should learn. Students are individuals and do not require the same abilities for all learners. Even in the area of reading it is uncertain as to which skills may one learner needs in order to read proficiently. Some need more phonics than others. Selected readers may learn to read well utilising the whole word method rather than phonetic analysis. In teaching, educators deal with individuals and not with groups or mass numbers of individuals. Students are human beings

and not machines. They "master" a skill and may forget it a short time later.

3. *Mastery learning:* No doubt, politics was involved when the concept of mastery, learning came into being in education. In learning skills as was stated previously, it may appear to the teacher that a skill, such as in using guide words in a dictionary is known or mastered. It may be that a few minutes later that the pupil has forgotten completely what is meant by guide words, let alone using the concept. Mastery learning sounds good, but educator and lay people need to understand the processes of learning more effectively.

4. *Competency based instruction:* This concept merely emphasises teachers teaching toward measurably stated objectives previously identified. The precise objectives may have been carefully or carelessly identified. After teaching, the teacher may measure if a pupil has/has not attained the precise objectives. The term *competency based* is greatly inflated in its value. It almost sounds as if other methods of teaching deemphasise competency models.

Administrators need to encourage teachers to utilise a variety of activities including:

1. textbooks, workbooks, encyclopaedias, and other reading materials;
2. audio-visual materials (films, filmstrips, slides, pictures, transparencies, study prints, excursions, as well as services of quality resources personnel;
3. computer assisted instruction (CAI) as well as using programmed textbooks for learners.

A variety of learning activities should be emphasised for the sake of doing so. Rather, the diverse kinds of materials utilised in teaching assist students individually to achieve as much as possible.

A third task for administrators is to assist teachers to develop a quality system of evaluating student progress. Evaluation is done to determine how much each pupil has learned. The teacher must know if pupils are learning as much as individual capacities and abilities permit. Students must be challenged to make as much progress as possible. But, it must be remembered that administrators and teachers should not have students attempt to learn that which is too complex and too difficult. Trivia and the irrelevant need to be culled from situations.

Now, back to the specific topic of evaluation. When student progress is being appraised, academic, social, emotional, and moral achievement needs to be noticed. Proper physical development also is significant for each student. Academic achievement alone, should not be emphasised. But, intellectual achievement is highly important along with social growth, such as students learning to get along well with each others in an effective manner. Just think of how damaging it would be to the learner to do well in academic learnings only and fail miserably in dealing harmoniously with other human beings. Or, how terrible it would be to achieve extremely well in the academic subject matter areas and yet lack appropriate moral guidelines which provide direction and purpose in life. Too frequently, national study groups have advocated excellence in education. Excellence according to these study groups means achieving extremely well in the academic domain only. The writer would like to warn against this line of thinking. For example, supposing that a student would achieve well in subject matter areas only and lack proper emotional achievement. After all, the emotions (feelings, values, and beliefs) of a person are highly significant. Negative feelings continuously exhibited by any one person can make life very unpleasant for others in society as well as for the involved person.

Further Cautions on Recommendations

There certainly are an excess number of recommendations coming out on how to improve the public schools. However, there is little agreement on how to improve the public school curriculum. One must issue cautions on the following:

1. an excess amount of faith placed upon test results to notice student progress. Statewide tests cost much money in their development and use. Could the money be utilised more effectively in other ways, such as buying updated textbooks and other teaching materials? It takes *much* time for teachers to be secretaries and record test results of students. Here, the time of the teacher could be utilised much more wisely by preparing for and implementing quality plans for teaching;
2. advocating developing better textbooks than are presently on the market. Too frequently, the lay public believes the more difficult it is for pupils such as printed content in textbooks, the better it is for learners. The writer would caution against the concept *the more complex something is, the better*. Better it would be if the lay public and educators advocate helping each student achieve as much as possible, but not frustrate students with unattainable goals;
3. "high expectancies for students." The writer would caution against parents, and administrators having expectancies which are unattainable for students. The dropout rate of pupils from schools might then be extremely high. Situations such as these would not solve problems pertaining to the student's individual future;
4. strong business-school partnerships. The business world represent the private sector which President Reagan holds in extremely high esteem. The public schools represent the public sector which cannot and must not emphasise the profit motive. Schools exist to aid each pupil to achieve as much as possible.

   Assistance the business world could provide to the public schools is to develop a quality curriculum for each learner. The business world must realise that they can learn much from the public schools. For example, the public schools must accept each student regardless of the quality involved. They (the schools) cannot shut down and move away when undesirable students are in the offing. Businesses, however, may close their doors and move to a foreign nation where cheaper labour can be secured in order to stay solvent or even to secure greater profits;

5. schools must give students the basic skills in order that the latter may get a job. That certainly is an unintelligent statement that a United States senator made. First of all, no one can *give* an education to others. Each must reach out and learn. If skills could be given, the writer would like to have those abilities possessed by leading scientists. Secondly, who can play the role of God to know which skills any one person might need in the future?

6. the principal needs to be a strong leader in the school due to "as the administrator is in his/her leadership—so is the achievement of students within the school." The above statement gives administrators an almost blank check to be dictators in improving the curriculum. Certainly, an administrator has a vital role to improve the curriculum. However, a hierarchical structure whereby *relevancy* in ideas moves only in the direction from the administrator to teachers is not recommended. Today's teacher is well educated, and, no doubt, does well in coping with negative situations, such as low salaries, unfortunate home environment of students, inadequate instructional materials in schools to provide for individual differences, and the ever present budget cutter on local school boards. Thus, administrators and teachers cooperatively need to develop a curriculum which truly assists each pupil to achieve as much as abilities will permit.

7. cost/benefit analysis is the key to effective practices in education. Thus, the cost of pupils' attaining each measurable objectives is computed. However, the

attained objective may represent trivia. There are learning attained which are highly significant and not measurable, such as creative thinking. Being able to think creatively has certainly changed society and made for positive improvements;

8. changes need to be made quickly in education. No statement is ever made in which direction(s) the modifications should go. The lay public and selected educators look to the past for goals and emphasise the tried and true basics to the emphasised in the school curriculum. Many educators, however, look forward the future in ascertaining objectives for student attainment. The goals emphasise a comprehensive curriculum, much broader than the basic (reading, writing, and arithmetic).

The writer wonders why major changes are not emphasised and made in the legal and the medical professions. Also, the financial institutions, the home, and elected officials need to appraise themselves, and come up with desired changes to benefit human beings in society.

In Closing

Teachers, supervisors, and parents need to establish worthwhile objectives for students to achieve. The goals selected need to be relevant and feasible for students to realise. Each student needs to achieve in an optimal manner.

12

Problem Solving and the School Administrator

Administrators in the school setting face diverse problematic situations. To most problems needing solutions, there are no right or wrong answers. Each problem is seemingly unique to the situation. Solutions to problems are not absolutes, but relative to the situation. Many persons desire simple solutions to complex problems. To be sure, selected minor problems are easy to solve. Others require depth data gathering to come up with needed solutions. Frequently, however, time is rather limited to come up with answers to complex problems.

Administrators need to be sensitive to identifying problems in the school environment. Problems exist and do need to be identified. Avoiding the identification of problems merely adds to troublesome situations in schools. Courage to face and identify problems is significant for school administrators. To improve the curriculum of a school or school system, identification of problematic situations is important. Adequate data needs to be gathered to solve a problem. Sometimes, on the spur of the moment, solutions to problems need implementation, such is in a current discipline problem. Hypotheses (answers) to problems are tentative and subject to testing. Too frequently, hypothesis perceived as being final and fixed. When hypotheses are tested, it is quite obvious that modification and change may be necessary. Thus, what works in one situation involving discipline may not work in a different case.

Administrators then need to be skilled in identifying and solving problems.

Discipline and the School Administrative

A major role of school administrators emphasises disciplining students for misbehaviour. A student is sent to the administrator's office for disrupting other students in the classroom, for sighting on the playground, for using profanity, for stealing, and other infractions of rules. A teacher may be weak in gaining the respect of students and sends more students to the principal's office as compared to other teachers in the school setting. A particular student who has behaved appropriately previously may change in behaviour. The behaviour changes may be due to loss of friends, to sickness or death of a person in the home setting, to neglect and abuse from the parent(s), and to feelings of general insecurity. An endless number of reasons can be listed for misbehaviour in the classroom, including the physical and mental health of the misbehaving student.

A knowledgeable administrator attempts to look at causes for misbehaviour. The cause(s) may be detectable or be numerous, complex, or not identifiable. Causes must still be carefully considered. Social literacy training as one concept in school discipline emphasises looking at causes from the point of view of the institution of the entire school or school system. Thus, there may be unnecessary and excessively strict rules. Rules and regulations in school need to be reasonable in number and in terms of quality standards. Existent rules should assist students to learn and to achieve. Sometimes, rules are there to show authority and power over students. The writer recommends strongly that principals and teachers look at the school and class setting to notice if standards of conduct being emphasised hinder student behaviour and achievement.

When causes reside within the school and classroom setting (extrinsic to the learner), a problem solving situation exists. A problem needs to be identified. Information must then be secured in answer to the clearly defined problematic situations. A hypothesis needs to be developed which is an answer to the problem. The hypothesis should be tested in action and revisions made if necessary. It is imperative for the school administrator and the teachers to utilise tenets of social literacy theory to minimise problems pertaining to discipline among students.

Problem solving is also necessary if situations of discipline reside within the student. How should infracture of responsible rules and regulations by students be handled? A systemwide discipline policy takes time to study, analyse, develop and implement. If, after careful study, the school administration and teachers decide upon utilising tenets of assertive discipline, responsible criteria to follow need to be identified and communicated clearly to students. Students must understand and attach meaning to these standards. Administrators and teachers also need to agree in a flexible manner, how to handle the first, second, and third infrastructures of a standard or standards before the parent(s) are called to school to talk with the teachers and administrator about the student's misbehaviour. Agreement then needs to be reached by the parent(s) and teacher, as well as principal, on how to minimise discipline problems for the involved situation.

Problem Solving and the Curriculum

A curriculum for students is not stable not static. A changing curriculum will be in evidence. Why? Society changes and these modifications are reflected within the school curriculum. A rather recent innovation in society—the use of the computer—has made for changes in media utilised to assist student learning. Each classroom of students taught by a teacher is different, in degree, from last years roomful of learners. Students, individually change physically, socially, emotionally, and socially, as they progress through the sequential years of schooling. With the many changes occurring in school and in society, the curriculum must also change.

There are numerous curricular problems for administrators and teachers to identify and solve. These include:

1. emphasising quality sequence in student learning;

2. stressing an integrated curriculum where desirable and feasible;
3. advocating scope (breadth of subject matter) which meets needs, interests, and purpose of students;
4. implementing balance among objectives, such as cognitive, affective, and psychomotor goals. Each of these objectives should be reflected within ongoing lessons and units;
5. favouring intensive, depth teaching rather than survey approaches in the classroom setting;
6. emphasising a variety of evaluation techniques to appraise various facets of understanding, skills, and attitudinal learnings acquired by students. In solving problems pertaining to curriculum, development, each student should be assisted to attain optimally.

School Attendance and the Principal

Excessive absences and tardiness can certainly hinder student progress. Teachers need to take more time to plan for what students have missed due to being absent or tardy. What has been planned by teachers needs to be implemented to take care of student deficiencies in sequential learning. The absent or tardy student should achieve new learnings rather than makeup that which has been missed or omitted on a previous day or days of school.

What can be done to minimise unnecessary absences and tardiness? Certificates may be given on a weekly, monthly, or yearly basis for good attendance. Extrinsic motivational devices are utilised in these situations to encourage regular student attendance. To vary the reward approach to emphasise students attending school regularly, inexpensive badges and prizes may be given at selected intervals. The extrinsic reward is contingent upon regular student attendance in school. The school administrator may conduct faulty meetings or a workshop in guiding teachers to use rewards systems to encourage student attendance.

No doubt, the best approach in emphasising good attendance by students is intrinsic motivation strategies. From within, students then have a desire to be in school and be there on time. Attitudes and feelings of learners reflect their desire to learn and to achieve. There are selected guidelines which may be utilised by teachers to develop student interest in learning. Thus, lessons and ongoing units should be exciting and challenging to students. Boring and routine learning activities need to be replaced. Each student experiences tasks which are interesting and fascinating. Drudgery is then not in evidence in curricular experiences for students. Students individually need to be successful learners. No one likes to experience failure. Rather, with success in learning, sequence is experienced by students. New facts, concepts, and generalisations achieved are based upon and related to previously acquired learnings.

Too frequently, teachers emphasise the utilisation of basal textbooks, workbooks, and worksheets as learning activities for students. Experiences in the classroom should also stress activity centred approaches in teaching and learning. The activity centred curriculum for students might well include dramatising what has been learned, constructing models and dioramas of previously acquired learning, developing a mural or individual pencil sketches pertaining to content attained, as well as write diverse kinds of prose and poetry reflecting subject matter learned. An increased use of audio-visual aids (slides, films, filmstrips, and transparencies) may further increase interest in learning; the rate of absenteeism and tardiness may go down, hopefully.

The school administrator and the teacher have definite problems to identify and solve involving improved school attendance on the part of students.

Problem Solving and Inservice Education

Administrators and teachers, as well as support personnel need to grow, learn, progress, and achieve. Inservice education can spur individuals on to greater levels of progress. The principal needs to identify problems in the area of inservice education for school personnel. Teachers also need to be involved in identifying and solving vital, relevant problems.

A school administrator emphasising a problem solving philosophy must show courage in stressing problem solving rather than the avoidance of identifying weaknesses and difficulties in the school and class setting. Democratic procedures need emphasis in that all who have a role in these problematic situations are involved in analysing and acquiring solutions to perplexities and conflicts in the educational arena.

Which problems need identifications and solutions through inservice education procedures? There might well be a need to emphasise peers helping other students achieve well in the classroom setting. An excessive number of students in any classroom makes it difficult to provide for individual differences among learners. Peer assistance in teaching individual students might well make it possible for the classroom teacher to spend more time with a specific set of students needing increased aid to achieve well in school. Inservice education sessions can emphasise the implementation of using peers in teaching other students.

Adult, paid or unpaid aides, may also do well in assisting the regular teacher to help students achieve optimally in the classroom. If aids do not assist teachers effectively, what needs to be done then? A problem has then been identified and needs solution. The principal and the teacher(s) need to clarify the problematic situation. A discussion is held to shed light on the problem. The discussion may be considered as a data gathering technique in securing information directly related to the problem. A related hypothesis should result. The hypothesis might involve and inservice education programme for teacher aides in the classroom. After the inservice programme has been completed, the hypothesis may need revising. Workshop results might also indicate that aides are doing a better job of assisting teachers in the classroom as compared to previous times. If aides are doing no better than formerly as a result of the inservice education programme, they may need to be replaced. Aides are in the classroom to assist teachers to provide adequately for students of diverse interest and achievement levels.

The administrator needs to be a proficient solver of problems at the building level, as well as in the entire school system.

Problem Solving and Personal Needs of Teachers

Teachers have personal needs which can be quite different as compared to institutional needs of the school. An administrator generally would not be a trained, licensed counselor. However, he/she can be sympathetic, have understanding, and show empathy to teacher needs. The human condition seemingly emphasises that people have personal problems. The best of individuals experience major as well as minor problems.

The writer, as a school principal, had an excellent combination room teacher for grades on and two. This teacher prepared well, worked effectively with young children, and got along well with other adults in the building. In August, three weeks before the new school year began, her husband left her. This teacher became distraught over the situation and resigned her position in this small rural city. Divorce seemingly can come to the best of individuals. Here was an excellent classroom teacher and divorce was shattering to her. Other people are not as overwhelmed with a divorce, but still experience trauma.

There are many other situations involving the human condition which truly hinder effective teaching. Numerous teachers have problems with aging parents. Selected teachers are very concerned about the welfare of parents who cannot take care of themselves properly. There is a drain of energy on the conscientious teacher's part in taking care of these parents. There can be a major decision which needs to be made in terms of home care versus care in a nursing home.

Death of a parent, child, husband or wife, can be another drain on the teacher's effectiveness in teaching. A sudden death from an automobile accident or heart attack takes its toll on human effectiveness. Lingering illnesses from cancer or strokes of a loved one certainly does affect how well a teacher teaches in the classroom. The writer was a fifth grader when his mother had a severely disabling stroke which left her paralysed on the left-hand side and made speaking very difficult. She died twenty-two years later. That is a long time to suffer a complex disability.

Runaway children indeed affect the teacher in many ways. The writer is acquainted with a teacher whose daughter ran away from home. This teacher mentioned how difficult it is to accept the fact that a child ran away from home. The community may be rude to the parent in these kinds of situations which add to stress in life. Fortunately, the daughter returned home. But, what happends to a good teacher's style of teaching with a missing child?

Child abuse is a common topic in the news. If a teacher's child is abused, certainly, the administrator needs to be empathetic and understanding. He/she needs to listen, understand, and be sympathetic of the human condition with its uninvited trails and tribulations.

There are a few additional human conditions, the writer wishes to enumerate:

1. What should be done where an excellent teacher's health has deteriorated and thus affects the quality of teaching? Does a school dismiss teachers who come in this category?
2. Selected teachers who do a good job of teaching experience intervals of depression. Should these teachers look for a different position, other than teaching since books with depression do affect teacher interaction with students?

The school administrator, as a problem solver, needs to realise the human condition. The human condition has its successes and failures. There are uninvited situations in life which affect the teacher negatively. These negative happenings definitely affect the quality of teaching in the classroom. The principal needs to develop and possess feelings of empathy toward teachers who experience the unfortunate at selected intervals in life. Being a good listener and desiring to help solve personal problems of teachers, the school administrator is indeed a highly valued person.

In Closing

The writer has attempted to enumerate definite instances in which the principal needs to have the knowledge, skills, and attitudes of wishing to solve problems. The goals of the institution (the school and school system) change rather continuously. Society has its rapid change rate. Schools cannot remain static but must incorporate desired, needed changes. Teachers and other school personnel also experience desired as well as undesired situations involving change. With change in school and in society, the school administrator needs to identify and hopefully solve relevant, vital problems.

13

Stay Current and Updated, Administrators

A major problem in the field of school administration is to maintain interest in this vital endeavour in education. One hears expressions such as the following pertaining to school administrators:

1. He/she is no longer interested in being a school administrator.
2. The administrator is holding on until retirement time.
3. The principal/superintendent does not want to rock the boat and thus is so uninnovative.
4. He/she locks the self in his/her office so that decisions do not need to be made.
5. The administrator shows ignorance and does not keep abreast of current trends in education.

There are school administrators who follow one or more of the above enumerated criteria year after year within a school system. There are receiving schools who hire these kinds of administrators for a variety of reasons. Situations, such as these, are sad indeed! Students in the school and class setting need to achieve and learn. Relevant objectives need to be attained by learners. A school administrator has a vital role to play in providing leadership to improve the curriculum. Important curricular decisions need to be made to assist each student to achieve in an optimal manner.

Maintaining Interest in School Administration

Education is continuous, ongoing, and should never cease during one's lifetime. There is no exception to this statement when it comes to the profession of educational administration. The explosion of knowledge continues to double each five to ten years. In the area of school administration, professional books, Journals, manuscripts, brochuers, leaflets, and other printed materials, as well as audio-visual materials, abound in numbers. It is truly difficult to keep up with current literature in school administration.

It behooves administrators of schools to develop and maintain interest in their professional careers. There needs to be ample opportunities among school administrators in a district to discuss relevant ideas in their field. Stimulating each other with new content can indeed be fascinating. Discussing issues such as career ladders, mastery learning, management by objectives, exit objectives, software and microcomputers in-school suspension, team learning an activity centred curriculum, textbook selection, problem solving sustained silent reading, among other innovations, as a definite fascination of its very own. In discussions among school administrators, modifications of these concepts and their adaptations to local teaching-learning situations are important. New content needs to be generated. Schools and school systems continually identify problems and need creative solutions to those problematic areas. Life in and of itself does not remain stable, but seemingly changes rather continuously. Each new day brings its problems, challenges, and rewards. With change being an important concept in school and society, interest needs to be there to deal with changing situations.

Attending professional meetings at the national, state and local levels can aid in developing and maintaining interest in school-administration. New ideas and novel ways of identifying and solving problems need to be experienced by school administrators. Being an administrator involves creative behaviour. Creativity comes in degrees. Some are more creative than others. A knowledge base is necessary for creative behaviour. These facts, concepts, and generalisations in part, may come from attending professional meetings. Hearing presentations on inquiry learning, hypotheses testing, and sequence in the curriculum may well provide food for thought and action for school administrators. Visiting with others, while attending professional meetings, can stimulate further thought and interest in education. What has been learned from attending professional meetings needs to be shared with other administrators, teachers, and support personnel in the local school district.

Faculty meetings and workshops should have as a goal the stimulation of interest on the part of participants. Thus, in faculty meetings within a school, agenda items need to be relevant not trivial, stimulating not boring, and purposeful not routine. The administrator may share with faculty members the chairing of the meetings. A rotation procedure may then be followed. Any faculty meeting should present new idea in education to participants. With a high level of interest in a faculty meeting, administrators and other participants should receive new ideas. It is people who make life zestful or boring. Certainly there are vital topics and problems to cover in a faculty meeting which secures the interest and purpose of its members. Topics and problems such as the following should meet these criteria minimising and preventing burnout of school personnel, achieving an adequate self concept, and working harmoniously with students. There should be definite information provided in faculty meeting agendas which have application values in school and in society.

Workshops also have their values in developing more fully functioning individuals. Workshop sessions devoted to the interest of the self, as well as school and society might include developing physical fitness, starting a new hobby, and working successfully with adults. The goal of workshops is to renew not stultify, as well as, to grow and not become stale. Self realisation on the part of the administrator and other participants makes for increased effort and motivation to perform well in the school and class setting.

Visiting innovative schools can make for interest in the profession of school administration. The administrator needs to select the types of innovations which are perceived to have value in improving the curriculum. The school administrator may desire to see and visit with personnel in desired magnet schools and discuss innovative procedures. Visiting with principals and superintendents to discuss management by objectives in specific school districts has its very own fascination. In visiting innovative schools, the school administrator may realise a higher energy level to improve the curriculum on the local level.

School-administrators should have ample opportunity to be involved in research studies. Individual or team effort may be involved in conducting research. Practical research should be stressed which is applicable to the local school setting. However, theoretical or pure research can also be a stimulator and motivator for administrators to participate in. With a carefully planned design, adequate assistance, materials and funding, research can be conducted which is useful as well as interesting. Effort is put forth in conducting research that is of interest to the school administrator.

Speaking at civic and professional meetings may well generate its very own interest. Being a speaker may well being out the best within the individual. The school administrator needs to practice the art and skill of speaking. Being able to present content which is especially interesting to the speaker can be stimulating and fascinating. Which topics might be of interest to the administrator in speaking at professional meetings? Certainly, trends and innovations in school administration can be of great interest. Reading and research is necessary to develop a talk pertaining to that which is emphasised and recommended in the area of school administration. The content of the talk may assist the involved administrator to appraise his/her own school/school system with that recommended from the ongoing research. To develop and remain a professional is the process of becoming and not a finished product.

Writing for publication may well develop and maintain interest in the professional of school administration. The content might come from research conducted and talks presented at diverse civic and professional meetings. Subject matter for writing might also come from personal experiences in everyday situations in school. Certainly, through writing and publication, the local administrator may share practical ideas with principals and superintendents in state, national and international journals. It is rewarding to publish and to share means of improving the administration of schools with other professionals. The writer has had upwards of 800 manuscripts in diverse facets of education published in the United States and abroad. One should not speak of publish or perish. Rather, the school administrator writes and publishes due to inherent interest in writing and the joy of being rewarded with published manuscripts!

Each school needs to have an administrator's open house. The purpose of this event in the school setting is for parents and interested lay citizens, as well as teachers and support workers, to meet the school administrator. This should be an informal event. Coffee and rolls (refreshments) should be served at this occasion. The focus on administrator's open house is to acknowledge the importance of school administration to improve the curriculum for each student. Politeness and consideration is a "must" in the open house. The achievements of the administrators may be announced over the loud speaker, as well as being posted outside the administrator's office. Conscientious school administrators give much of themselves for others. Recognition for these services is a must in any community. The writer recommends that teachers and other school personnel be responsible for refreshments, notices, and announcements of the administrator's open house which should be an annual event.

Closely related to the open house concept is administrator's week. This event is modelled after secretary's week. The writer has often wondered why secretary's week is promoted, rather than administrator's week. To be sure, both are important. A quality secretary (or secretaries) is a must. So is the administrator of one or more schools. The school administrator needs to provide leadership which promotes optimal student progress. Why should administrators not be rewarded for being responsible leaders in education? Thus, during administrators' week, teachers and school personnel could plan something special for each day of that week. These might include flowers, a dinner, special recognition in an assembly programme, a certificate of achievement, and a box of candy. These rewards should assist the administrator to develop and maintain interest in truly being a professional educational leader.

In Closing

A highly valuable person in the school setting is the administrator. He/she can give much of themselves to assist students to learn, grow, and achieve. There also needs to be feedback to the school administrator in application for professional services rendered. The reward approach to maintain and increase interest in leadership roles include adequate opportunities for administrators to:

1. Discuss interesting, vital means to improve the curriculum.
2. Attend professional conferences and conventions in the area of school administration.
3. Conduct faculty meetings to consider purposeful items on the agenda.
4. Attend workshops which contain content of personal interest.
5. Visit innovative schools which capture the attention of the school administrator.
6. Participate in appealing, useful research studies.
7. Speak at professional meetings.
8. Write for publication in educational journals.
9. Participate in school administration open house.
10. Enjoy administration week in the school and community setting.

14

Leadership in Education

A major question that needs answering in the United States pertains to who should provide leadership and guidance in America education.

A barrage of criticisms have been hurled at current situations in public schools. Teachers have been criticised for (a) not teaching the basics. The basics generally are perceived as being the three R's —reading, writing, and arithmetic. Certainly a three R's curriculum is too narrow indeed and will not prepare students to live in a world of science and social problems, (b) not being competent in teaching in numerous situations. This would be difficult to substantiate. Class size and disrupters certainly hinder any teacher's effort to teach well. Competency tests are to be passed in many states prior to certifying new teachers. A passing mark has to be secured prior to licensing a teacher to teach in the public schools. The writer sees little relationship between being able to pass a test and doing a quality job of teaching. Certainly, a teacher should know basic subject matter which will be taught to pupils. However, it is doubtful if a test will measure adequately a teacher's ability to teach, (c) not having the kind of discipline in a classroom which society approves. Public schools by law must accept all students. Each pupil must receive an appropriate education. Thus, it is only likely that severe discipline problems will arise. Society has, of course, much greater offenders, as compared to the public schools, such as murderers, arsonists, thieves, robbers, among others. One cannot separate school from society. The societal arena therefore cannot expect an immaculate class and school environment. However, school boards and the lay public must provide an adequate supply of teachers to teach behavioural disorders students, as well as slow, average, and fast learners. School boards too long have rallied around the slogan, "Let's cut the budget". Rather, teachers of school boards should work in the direction of providing the best education possible for each student. Quality education is expensive. But quality education pays. The defense department keeps asking for the receives increased amounts of money. The Soviet Union, however, should not be perceived as being the basis enemy. Ignorance, illiteracy unemployment, poverty, and pollution, no doubt have greater enemies.

Schools boards should adopt the slogan, "Let's provide the best education possible", rather than "Let's cut the budget." No doubt, completely new approaches have seeded to finance American education as compared to present procedures which need modifying and overhauling.

Responsibilities of Schools

An excessive number of responsibilities have been hurled upon public schools. This has been true since the lay public has shirked where it should have taken the bull by the horns. Which tasks have not received its due attention by parents and guardians in society? There include:

(a) taking care of nutrition needs of students. Then noon meal for pupils has been served for many years in the public schools. Selected schools also serve breakfast since many parents are negligent in taking care of nutritional needs of their offspring.

    Certainly, public schools do not want to have lunchrooms. However, if students are to learn and achieve, food needs must be met by the public schools. There is no alternative.

(b) neglecting pupils in terms of clothing needs. If students come to schools with clothes that are excessively tight and do not close where needed, the public schools need to provide for appropriate and clean clothing. Otherwise, the neglected will be shunned by other pupils. Achievement in the three R's (reading, writing, and arithmetic), as well as other curriculum areas can then not take place from neglected students;

(c) abusing children through physical, sexual, and emotional abuse. Teachers, among other school personnel, are asked to contact appropriate authorities if abuse of a student has been in evidence. Reporting abused pupils to proper authorities can backfire to involved teachers. The presents can retaliate against the teacher or teachers who reported child abuse cases.

Reporting possible child abuse cases is not a delightful thing for teachers to do. Thus, another responsibility has been cast upon teachers and the public school;

(d) counselling services to pupils. There are numerous counsellors in the public schools, although greatly inadequate in terms of quality counsellors. Why do public schools provide counselling services? Certainly, it's not due to promising pie in the sky by and by. Rather, students come from unwanted homes. Negative home situations make for many problems in society. Poverty, unemployment, and divorce make for undesired situations in a home setting. Thus, the lay public wanted schools to counsel pupils. There, of course, are students who need sympathetic adults in school. Certainly a good counsellor can provide this understanding and support;

(e) having pupils acquire Biblical teachings and attitudes of prayer. The writer feels the present momentum of fundamentalist ministers, corgressman, senators, and the President to advocate integrating religion with the public schools is due to a lack of Biblical knowledge and knowledge of prayer among students. Homes and churches, among other groups, have definitely not provided this knowledge to their offspring.

When in the United States House of Representatives, the United States Senate, among other political situations, it is advocated that the Bible presents answers to all questions and problems faced by human beings, a traditional patriotic slogan is in evidence. It would be interesting to know how much Biblical knowledge, politicians truly possess. It probably would be very minimal. No doubt, as a personal opinion, the writer believes that the lay public wants students to learn more from the Bible and its teachings. Thus, the public schools with its compulsory attendance laws is a place to make up this deficiency.

Remedying Deficiencies

How might the previously stated deficiencies be remedied? No doubt, more responsibilities will be hurled on the public schools to cure societal ills. In sequence as was listed above, the public schools could do the following:

(a) to teach the basics and the curriculum areas more thoroughly, smaller class sizes for teachers to teach need to be in evidence. The writer firmly believes that if a teacher teaches above than twenty in a classroom, each pupil will not learn to read, write, and compute adequately. The more pupils are placed in a classroom, the more difficult it becomes to help each pupil do well in any subject matter area. There are research studies that say there is no relationship between class size and how well pupils do in reading, writing, and arithmetic. This is ridiculous! Why not place 2,000 pupils then with a single classroom teacher? Society could then really "save money." Any person should know that even the best of teachers could not assist a large number of students to achieve in any classroom. The writer believes a 15 pupils to one teacher is a good ratio, providing that disrupters do not exist in the classroom. A single disrupter should count as three students. Thus, to teach a set of disrupters, a five student to one teacher ration should suffice. Quality teaching costs much money. But the investment is excellent if the United States wishes to again become a world leader. Hopefully, this world leadership will deemphasise militarism and weapons build up. A positive nation in world leadership should have the best educational system possible, quality medical care and hospitals, excellent and safe roads and bridges, and achieving workers in society.

(b) to improve teaching competency, salaries of teachers in general should be raised fifty per cent. How many quality teachers will enter the profession of teaching with a beginning salary of $ 12,000? Not many. Any way, teachers need to earn a leviable salary so they do not need to moonlight or need foodstamps and free school lunches for their offspring. It's a sad commentary when school board members and the lay public state that "teachers need to be dedicated and not teach for money," or "teachers knew that salaries would be low when they entered teaching." So why should teacher's salaries be raised? If a teacher is to reveal dedication only and not receive a leviable salary, the writer wonders why all professionals and nonprofessionals aren't dedicated only and show no interest in earning money, doctors, dentists, and lawyers included.

Thus, adequate salaries for teachers need to be in the offing to attract quality individuals into teaching.

(c) to improve the quality of home life in order that child abuse is minimised, public schools need to take on more responsibilities. These tasks are not welcomed by schools. Rather, they are hurled upon the public schools. Thus, the public schools need to provide instruction and learning in parenting. To achieve appropriate standards in being quality parents is a difficult task indeed. Here, the public schools cannot make guarantees. Definite objectives cannot be established pertaining to parenting. Educators and the lay public must realise that public schools cannot, by any means, guarantee success in guiding parents to do a quality job of parenting. Generally, the public schools will do the best possible under involved circumstances.

No professional or agency can guarantee a miracle. If miracles were possible, why aren't the following achieved?

1. full employment in society;
2. no prisoners in prisons;
3. zero juvenile delinquency;
4. no automobile accidents;
5. fairness in court trials and legal procedures. There are tremendous weakness here in the profession of law;
6. successful surgery in all cases and perfection in medical care.

Newsreporters and the news media, as well as educators (usually ambitious professors), should not report weaknesses that are so minor in education that human beings cannot presently remedy. When evaluating the quality of public education in the United States, reasonable standards only (not the impossible) should be stressed. In other words, no teacher or school can have each student achieve as much as his/her abilities permit because:

1. the exact upper limits of any one pupil is not known;
2. learners become tried and turn off at intervals;
3. adequate materials in a classroom do not exist to guide optimal individual achievement;
4. a single teacher cannot teach a set of 20 to 25 students so each achieves as much as possible. There, of course, will be times when a student hears that which is repetitious or too complex.

(d) to improve counselling services, adequate money needs to be available to hire quality counsellors, adequate in number. Budget cutters in schools have eliminated many counselling positions. Frequently, there are zero counsellors on the elementary school level. And yet, if homes do not accept responsibilities for raising and educating children, the public school is left holding the bag for these significant tasks. Again, it can truly be said that quality education and related services do cost much money. However, the United States is needed a wealthy, definitely not a poor nation, and can afford quality education for each student. A number of years ago, the writer say poverty and misfortune in its ultimate. That was when he whitewashed caves for Palestinian refugees on the West Bank of the Jordan River. That was truly a catastrophe and tragedy with hopelessness and a lack of the good things in life for the Palestinians. Being a refugee is an demeaning as any situation in life can be. But, the United States possesses wealth in abundance and can provide the best in education for each student. The answer in quality education does not lie in reducing taxes for the wealthy in particular, nor in "that government is best which governs least." Governmental rules and regulations must exist in order to provide an education which meets needs of each students. "Let's get government off our backs and out of our pockets" will definitely make for an inferior system of education. The Defence Department does not advocate the previous slogan. They advocate increased funding. The public schools also must advocate moneys need to develop the best school system in the world.

(e) to emphasise Bible reading and prayer in the public schools necessitates providing for individual differences among students. Students come from diverse religious backgrounds. Even within the protestant faith, there are extreme difference in religious thinking such as the mode of baptism (sprinkling or immersion), faith (beliefs, such as the triune God) versus works (feeding and clothing the hungry as well as visiting the sick), and using military might against the enemy (fundamentalist evangelical beliefs) versus pacifism (Mennonites and Quakers, as example).

Thus, the rights of students and their parents must be respected if Bible reading and prayer in the public schools were emphasised. It is not as simple then to advocate that all protestant students should have the freedom to utter protestant prayers, since grave differences in religious beliefs exist among the diverse groups and sects. It, no doubt, would be easier to provide for all Catholic students within a group as compared to the diverse faiths in the Protestant religion.

Those professing no religious preference or being opposed to any religious might well be involved in a class dealing with moral issues and their resolutions. These problems in the morality area could include the pros and cons of capital punishment, abortion, military solutions to international problems, as well as employment versus inflation in American society.

In Closing

Many responsibilities have been hurled upon the public schools. These tasks were not involved. However, the educational arena make take care of deficiencies if other institutions are unwilling or unable to do so.

No doubt, as the years elapse, increased responsibilities will be given to the public schools. These will include:

(a) increased emphasis upon integration of the races due to society having failed miserably in this area.

Thus, busing of students magnet schools, among other procedures will continually be utilised.

(b) responsibilities for taking care of latch key children, unwanted children, school dropouts, and unwed pregnant teenagers.

(c) major emphasis placed upon educating adults who are illiterate. There are selected adults who did not apply themselves while being students in the public schools.

(d) increased health services for students in schools. Due to neglect or poverty of parents, the public schools will need to survey and screen students in the area of dental hygiene, mental hygiene, and physical health. Perhaps, the public schools will need to go beyond surveying and screening in the health arena, by actually providing eye glasses, hearing aids, and suitable clothing, as well as needed medical and dental services.

The above needs of students must be taken care of so that each learner may achieve as optimally as possible.

15

Discipline and the School

Teachers and administrators are concerned about the quality of discipline in the school/class setting. There is fear that learners may and do get out of hand. Learning on the part of students is hindered. The quality of education then goes downhill.

Toward the other end of the continuum, discipline may be excessively strict! Students are reluctant to be active participants in ongoing experiences. Less creativity is in evidence then from structures. It appears that a Golden Mean should be emphasised in discipline. Thus, an environment can be excessively permissive. Or, strictness as a concept is being emphasised rather than are students truly learning and achieving.

The Psychology of Learning

There are selected principles of learning which need emphasis in the curriculum. Otherwise discipline problems might arise due to ineffective methods of teaching and learning being emphasised in ongoing units of study.

1. Purpose in Learning

The teacher needs to develop or maintain purpose for learning within pupils. Pupils may learn very little from ongoing learning activities if they "see" little or no purpose in what is being learned. Learners must sense a reason for learning selected facts, concepts, and generalisations. Too frequently, the classroom teacher has merely assigned a certain number of pages for pupils to read from a textbook with no readiness activities involving purpose for reading. The teacher, perhaps, merely stated the following: "read pager 110 to 113 for tomorrow and answer questions five, six, and seven at the end of the chapter." It is no wonder that many learners fail to sense purpose for reading.

If pupils are to read content from a basal reader, for example, the teacher can guide pupils in a discussion pertaining to the related pictures in the textbook. Pictures from the teacher's file could also be utilised. As these pictures are being discussed, the teacher could print the related new words on the chalkboard that pupils will be encountering in their reading. These words should be printed in neat manuscript style and their meaning discussed. Pupils can then obtain a mental image of these words from the chalkboard and utilise these learnings in recognising new words which they will meet in print. They should also be able to recall the meanings of the new words when reading so that meaningful learning may take place. As the pictures and related new words are being discussed, pupils should ask questions and identify problem areas. Pupils can then read to find information to answer these questions or problem areas. Thus, a purpose is involved in learning than if no reasons exist for participating in a given learning activity.

2. Interest in Learning

It is important for teachers to select learning activities which capture the interests of pupils. Pupils should learn more if they are interested in a given learning activity as compared to having a lack of interest. Too often, teachers have not considered the interests of pupils when selecting appropriate learning activities. Thus, learners do not achieve to their optimum. The teacher can construct an interest inventory whereby pupils can respond in checking what is of interest to them. For example, on this interest inventory, all pupils could check their hobby or hobbies from those listed by the teacher. Space should be left for writing in their hobby or hobbies if they are not listed. Hobbis which pupils have can become a definite part of ongoing learning activities in a given unit. For example, stamps from a collection, pertaining to a unit of study on Great Britain, can become a part of the learning activities on that country. Or, a rock collection could become a definite part of a science unit pertaining to the changing surface of the earth. On the interest inventory, some pupils may indicate positive attitudes toward listening to music of other lands. Certainly these musical recordings can be brought into selected social studies units when they relate to the nations or areas of the world being studied. Teachers need to study various interest inventories and develop an instrument which would give data on ways of capturing the interests of pupils.

Pupils, generally, will show little interest in a given learning activity which is excessively complex. For example, pupils who read well below grade level will not be interested in reading content from books which are written for the grade level they are presently in. The words, terms, and ideas being presented from these textbooks will not be on the understanding level of pupils. Thus, interest in learning will lag. Nor will talented and gifted learners generally be interested in content which is written well below their present achievement level in reading. These learners will generally be bored and feel a lack of challenge in learning activities which have excessively low standards.

Some learning activities have a tendency to capture pupils interest more as compared to other kinds of activities. Well selected films, filmstrips, pictures, slides, excursions, and records can generate much pupil interest if properly introduced. Pupils from different achievement levels in a group can generally benefit from these learning activities. They can interpret and gain content on different achievement levels.

Learning activities involving discussions can make for a lack of interest on the part of learners, if the ideas being discussed contain excessively difficult vocabulary terms which learners do not understand or if the discussion activity is carried on for too long a period of time.

3. Meaning Attached to Learning

To benefit adequately from ongoing learning activities, pupils need to understand that which is being learned. Too frequently, pupils have memorised facts, statements, and conclusions without really understanding or attaching meaning to what has been learned. Or, pupils have memorised content for a test resulting in a rapid rate of forgetting. If pupils attach meaning to what has been learned, an improved retention rate should thus result. All teachers should be highly interested in having pupils retain as much as possible of what has been learned.

For learning to be meaningful for pupils, the teacher must assess the learner in terms of his present achievement level. Thus, in initiating or introducing a unit, the teacher should develop some kind of protest which will assist in determining present achievement levels of pupils. This could involve the use of variety of evaluation techniques. Paper-pencil tests could be used as well as discussions. No all evaluation, of course, should be done through the use of paper-pencil tests. Tests such as these will not adequately measure how well pupils can utilise a microscope in science or how well pupils can construct and make models related to ongoing social studies units.

Once pupils have been protested, the teacher needs to adjust objectives in a unit of study. The objectives should then be attainable for pupils. Careful selection of learning activities or determining an appropriate instructional sequence for learners is then important. If the objectives are too difficult for pupils to realise, meaningful learnings will then not occur. Learning activities which are too difficult for pupils make for a lack of meaningful learnings on the part of children. The teacher needs to pay careful attention to proper sequence when pupils are pursuing ongoing learning activities. The teacher may "jump" too far ahead of pupils if careful attention is not paid to proper sequence in ongoing learning activities. The other extreme in sequence could pertain to the teacher duplicating what learners already have mastered or learned in previous units of study. Thus, it is important that the teacher think in terms of good sequence when providing learning activities for pupils.

The teacher can be misled in providing for meaningful learning activities for pupils if the type of pretest utilised is not in harmony with the learner's present achievement level. For example, a first grade pupil will not reveal present achievement level, generally, if he were asked to read and respond to complex true-false, multiple-choice, completion or matching items. Each child must be pretested using an appropriate evaluation, technique which is in harmony with child growth and development characteristics.

4. Motivating the Learner

Pupils who lack motivation will not have the necessary energy level to become actively involved and benefit fully from ongoing learning activities. The teacher must think of strategies which assist learners to achieve to their optimum due to appropriate motivation. Forcing learners to memorise a given set of facts, generally, would make for situations where learners lack motivation. In some situations, teachers want to depend upon scolding or embarrassing learners in order to "encourage" learning. Sooner or later, teachers discover that under such circumstances pupils learn to dislike learning, teachers, as well as the school as an institution. Pupils may come to the conclusion that school is an unhappy place and learning is something to be shunned. A few teachers still feel that pupils learn only when they are forced to and that learning occurs only in situations involving drudgery. These teachers may think and feel that learning cannot be enjoyable for children and in their deeds emphasises that "learning" can come about largelly when experiences for children are made unpleasant through regurgitation of facts, rote learning, and drill.

The teacher rather needs to think of stimulating pupils so that an inward desire to learn will result. A good bulletin board development at different intervals when units are taught can do much to assist pupils in asking questions whereby a desire exists to get data in answer to these questions. In developing these bulletin board displays, the teacher needs to think of possible questions pupils may raise pertaining to the pictures contained thereon. Can the bulletin board display help develop an inward desire to learn on the part of pupils? This question needs to be answered in an affirmative by classroom teachers. The teacher can also develop interesting learning centres pertaining to different units of study. This should assist learners in identifying important problem areas thus motivating pupils in developing an inward desire to learn. The teacher can also utilise films and filmstrips containing content which would stimulate pupil curiosity. Learning activities need to be selected carefully by teachers so that pupil motivation for learning will be at its optimum.

Methods of Disciplining Students

In effective methodology has been utilised in teaching students and discipline problems persist, which alternatives are available to the teacher and administrator?

1. Using reinforcement tactics. Reinforcement emphasises using praise prizes, free time, tokens to exchange for prize, notes of commendation, recognition in all school assemblies, badges and certificates for improved learner performance. The teacher needs to determine the amount any student needs to learn and communicate this to involved learners, prior to any given learning opportunities. Thus, if it is reasonable for a learner to spell fifty words correctly within a given time interval, what will be the reward? Or, if a student does not disturb others within a specific interval of time, which reinforcement tactic will be utilised? Each learner needs to know what to achieve within a time interval in order to receive an award or prize. In a precise and clear manner, the teacher needs to communicate what is desired from each student in order that the learner may work in the direction of receiving positive reinforcement.

Biehler wrote the following involving reinforcement theory (S-R view and the thinking of B.R. Skinner).

The underlying philosophy of the S-R view stresses that scientists have been most successful when they have traced the causes of events and have found ways to alter behaviour in predictable ways. To apply science to human behaviour, therefore, Skinner argues that we must constantly analyse causes. If we can discover what makes people behave in a desirable manner, we should be able to arrange conditions to produce that kind of behaviour. If we do not search for courses and attempt to arrange experiences, we will leave things to chance. In an uncontrolled situation some lucky individuals will have a favourable chain of experiences that will equip them with desirable attitudes and skills, others will suffer an unfortunate series of experiences that will lead to difficulties and grief. In a controlled situation it may be possible to arrange experiences so that almost everyone acquires desirable traits and abilities.

Even if you feel a bit uncomfortable about the idea that human behaviour is shaped by experiences over which the individual has incomplete control. Skinner argues that you will be a better teacher if you endorse this assumption. If you reject the proposal completely, you may not become aware of how you are influencing your pupils in undesirable ways, and you may fail to arrange experiences that could benefit them. S-R theorists stress the point that what you do as a teacher-whether you acknowledge the fact or not-is going to have an impact on your students. Therefore, they recommend that you make systematic efforts to influence student behaviour in efficient, consistent, and positive ways.

2. Using satiation methods. If a disruption occurs in the classroom, the teacher may in an objective manner have the involved learner demonstrate for

an interval of time the disruptive behaviour. The assumption here is that the student will become tired of exhibiting negative behaviour. It may not be as enjoyable to perform what is negative when the student is encouraged in an open manner to do so. Generally, the pleasures of performing disruptive behaviour involves doing what the teacher disapproves of.

Thus, if two students have passed notes to each other during class time, they may be encouraged to do so during an interval of time so that classmates may observe the ensuring behaviour. Hopefully, the involved students will not engage in the disruptive behaviour in the future, i.e. passing notes during class time. The joy of doing so may be eliminated through satiation methods. If sanitation methods do not appear to work, other means of disciplining learners need to be utilised. Learners tend to exhibit those behaviours which appear to reward the personal self. There is no one proven method which works for all students in the area of discipline.

3. Using student-teacher planning. Each class of learners with teacher guidance may develop classroom standards of behaviour. Each criteria needs to be appraised in terms of developing recommended standards of behaviour within students. Thus, is the discussed criteria too lenient? Or, is it excessively stringent whereby harmful side effects could occur? It truly is a problem solving situation to develop recommend standards of behaviour.

After the criteria have been developed in a meaningful manner, they need implementation. If a learner breaks a rule, the class needs to discuss what the consequences of the infracture are. Should the adopted criteria not work, students with teacher guidance need to develop modified or new standards. Each standard is a hypothesis to be tested in the classroom setting. The consequences of any one standard is tested in action in the classroom setting. Only if the consequences are negative, should be criteria be revised. What is good in terms of standards is that which works in action. What is not effective produces nonworkable results. The world of experience is the real world. What exists in the experienced world is not stable not static, but changes. With change, new problems arise. These problems need identification are related solutions sought. Solutions are tentative and subject to change, if evidence warrants.

Preston and Hermann wrote:

Group formulation of rules or standards is desirable ("only four children may be at the reference table at a time"); "committees at work-keep your voices low"; and so on). There is evidence that children even as young as kindergarten age can participate in making and helping maintain rules.

Students should understand that the purpose of abiding by rules is not to please or ingratiate the teacher, but to create the kind of classroom in which learning can take place. Once the rules are made, discussed, and accepted, they should be posted and frequently referred to. The teacher should encourage the pupils to improve or add to them as the year proceeds.

4. Using modelling. The teacher may properly introduce and show a film to learners in which quality ideals in discipline are being emphasised. The content in the film should be realistic and not represent unachievable standards. Ultimately, the subject matter in the film may be discussed with involved learners. The purpose of the film is to present positive models for students to emulate. Each student models himself/herself after other admired individuals.

The teacher may also praise one or more students by name for exhibiting appropriate behaviours (reinforcement theory).

The rewarded learners provide models for others to imitate. The more prestigious the model, the more likely others will attempt to emulate that ideal. Notice in either example provided above, the teacher did not force the model or learners. Rather, the model is there for observation, imitation, and emulation.

Woolfolk and Nicolich wrote the following examples of modelling:

1. *Model those behaviours you want your students to learn examples:* Show enthusiasm for the subject you teach. Be willing to demonstrate the tasks you expect the students to perform.
2. *Use Peers as models examples:* In group work pair students who do well with those who are having difficulties. Ask students to explain lessons to the class or to a small group.
3. Make sure that students see that positive behaviours lead to reinforcement for others examples: Point out the connection between positive behaviour and positive consequences in stories. When a student is misbehaving, try to find another student near by who can be reinforced for behaving more appropriately.

In Summary

There are numerous means available to teachers and administrators to prevent or minimise discipline problems. First of all, each teacher needs to appraise the quality of his/her teaching in terms of recommended criteria from the psychology of learning. Discipline problems, of course, might arise if the teacher is not providing for individual differences.

After individual differences have been provided for adequately and problems in student behaviour are still in evidence, the teacher may try:

1. Reinforcement tactics by rewarding positive learner behaviour.
2. Student-teacher planning of standards of conduct in the classroom setting.

3. Satiation methods to convince learners that negative behaviour can be emphasised until the involved student becomes tired of its exhibition.

4. Modelling desired behaviour using audio-visual materials or quality student behaviour in the classroom.

REFERENCES

Anita H. Woolfolk and Lorraine McCune Nicolich. *Educational Psychology for Teachers*. Englewood Cliffs, New Jersey: Prentice Hall, Inc., 1980, Page 149.

Ralph C., Preston and Wayne Herman, Jr. *Teaching Social Studies in the Elementary School*. Fifth Edition. New York: Halt, Rinehart and Winston, 1981, Page 108.

Robert F., Biehler, *Psychology Applied to Teaching*. Third Edition. Boston: Houghton Mifflin Company, 1978, Page 229.

16

Staff Development Programmes

Much is written in educational literature pertaining to staff development. It appears that writers stress staff development for each innovation presented. For example, if the interdisciplinary curriculum needs emphasis, then staff development is needed. Or, if full inclusion is wanted, then staff development should be in evidence. I believe the first issue in staff development is how many sessions should be devoted to staff development when writers bring in new ideas in teaching and at the same time advocate staff development for implementing that idea. Is it necessary to have staff development for each new or innovative idea adopted in teaching and learning? Might teachers be trusted with implementing the new concept(s) on their own?

Further Issues in Staff Development

Who should determine what should be emphasised in staff development? A common vision is being emphasised as to what our schools should be like as a result of this vision. How is the vision to be achieved? A staff development programme, in part, may help. Ediger (1988) recommends that staff development programmes have three integrated parts such as a general session, small group or committee endeavours, and individual study. Teachers here should determine what is to be emphasised in the general session to identify problem areas, they should volunteer as to which committee to work on to solve problems, and then work individually on a problem of their very own choosing. The teacher and teaching here are at the centre of the stage in staff development. Principals and supervisors are there to assist teachers in working toward solutions of problem areas.

Toward the other end of the continuum, supervisors and principals after consultation with teachers, may desire to bring in a certain programme whereby staff development is necessary. The teachers are trained and educated to use a certain model in teaching after a quality programme of training. This approach at staff development has unique features that the first did not possess. The latter procedure in staff development is more principal/supervisor oriented, even though there was consultation with teachers about the new approach. Second, a commercial approach or one proposed by a team of educators was emphasised. The ideas for problem areas to be solved basically did not come from local teachers. Third, teachers must develop into having completely new teaching styles. The teaching model selected for staff development and implementation might not intrinsically be wanted by teachers. There may be a different procedure in teaching desired by teachers. Fourth, an external training team may be involved in the training of teachers. Trainers then come from outside the local school system or district. Fifth, trainers sequence experiences for teachers in staff training sessions. A logical approach is then involved in sequencing experiences for trainees.

What Should Training Sessions Stress?

The objectives of instruction may be changed or modified. Generally, cognitive objectives have received major emphasis in the curriculum. There are different levels of pupil achievement in the cognitive domain. Changes may be made from stressing the lower level cognitive objectives to those emphasising higher levels of thinking. Bloom's (1956) is still popular in discussing objectives form the lower to higher levels of cognition. His sequence is the following: recall of factual information by learners, comprehension of what has been recalled, application or using what has been learned, analysis involving official thought, synthesis stressing unique ways of putting the information together after analysis, and evaluation of what has been learned in terms of standards or criteria. Staff development programmes may stress teachers having children move for lower to higher cognitive objectives using Bloom's taxonomy. Learning opportunities need to be designed to guide pupils in thinking at a more complex level of ongoing learning opportunities. Feedback from teachers to members of the staff development programme should be in the offing after the teacher has used higher cognitive objectives in the classroom.

There is much discussion in education about having pupils apply what has been learned. Perhaps, a staff development programme will stress the level of application in ongoing training sessions. Teachers then put to use ideas developed and acquired in the staff development programme in the regular classroom. These teachers report back to the training session how the ideas worked out in the classroom.

Modification of objectives stressed in teaching and learning may also emphasise minimising cognitive and advocating affective ends in teaching. Affective objectives put more emphasis upon attitudes that pupils need to develop. Hopefully, quality attitudes will assist pupils to achieve cognitive objectives more effectively. Krathwohl stressed five levels of affective objectives in moving from the lowest to the higher levels. These are the following: paying attention to relevant content presented, responding to content with feeling or emotion, responding to content in a value oriented way, organising values and feelings into a structure, and characterising the attitudes in terms of being consistent and following a pattern. A quality affective curriculum emphasises pupils developing positive feelings and values.

A learning stations philosophy might well stress an affective curriculum. Here, the teacher together with pupils develop an adequate number of stations as well as tasks for each station. Pupils might then choose which tasks to complete and which to omit. Decision-making by learners is important. Ideally, pupils choose tasks which possess interest and perceived purpose. Motivation for learning should be higher if the pupil has had input into what he/she has planned and wishes to learn. The learner also is involved in planning and selecting—two concepts which no doubt are at the heart of democratic thinking. The learners chooses form among alternatives and he/she is affected by choices made, from among alternatives. Involvement by pupils in selecting objectives, learning activities, and appraisal procedures emphasises increasingly democratic living. Also the attitudes of the pupil determine, in part, what will be learned. A psychological curriculum stresses pupils sequencing their very own learning opportunities; opposite of a psychological curriculum is a logical curriculum whereby a teacher arranges the order of learning for pupils.

In noticing that an almost complete absence of statements advocating democracy and democratic ideals from policy makers, Fenstermacher (1995) write the following:

...We hear a great deal about readying the next generation of workers for global competition, about being first in the world in such high statues subjects as math and science, and about having world class standards for what is learned in school. We hear almost nothing about civic participation or building and maintaining democratic communities, whether these be neighbourhoods or governments at the local, state, or federal levels. The advancement of democratic ideals and institutions goes largely unmentioned, taken for granted or insufficiently important to rank up there with such world-shaking events as our playing Avis to Japan's Hertz.

Workshops and staff development programmes might then be arranged for the teacher to stress democracy as a way of life with the inclusion of affective objectives.

A third change in the curriculum may reflect may reflect the use of psychomotor objectives. Here, the school curriculum stresses the use of the gross and finer muscles of the learner. Harrow (1972) listed six levels of psychomotor objectives. These are the following:

1. reflex movement;

2. basic fundamental movements, including locomotor, non-locomotor manipulative movements;
3. perceptional abilities containing several subcategories:
   (a) kinesthetic discrimination that refers to body awareness, body image, body relationship of surrounding objects in space.
   (b) visual discrimination including visual awareness, visual tracking, visual memory, figure ground differentiation, and perceptual constancy.
   (c) auditory discrimination including auditory activity, tracking and memory.
   (d) tactile discrimination.
   (e) coordination.
4. physical abilities including enduring, strength, flexibility and agility.
5. skilled movement including simple adaptive skill, compound and complex adaptive skill;
6. non-discursive communication including expressive movements and interpretive movements.

In emphasising psychomotor objectives, the teacher assists pupils to become actively involved in making, constructing, artistic endeavours, doing and other forms of using physical movement and motion Psychomotor objectives may be used in any curriculum area and receive more emphasis in teaching and learning as compared to cognitive and affective ends of instruction (Earnest, 1995).

Staff development programmes may be needed to change from a cognitive or affective objectives emphasis to one stressing the psychomotor domain. Psychomotor objectives truly emphasise an activity centred curriculum for pupils. I surprise student teachers and regular teachers in the public school setting. In teaching a unit on "Weather and How It Affects Us," pupils with teaching team guidance discussed and constructed a barometer, a wind vane, a hygrometer, and an anemometer. Each object was goal centred, planned, constructed, and appraised in terms of criteria.

Learning Opportunities to Achieve Objectives

In changing from previously used activities and experiences to a new approach takes effort, knowledge, skill and motivation. If pupils are to use modern technology in the curriculum, it may truly revolutionise the curriculum depending upon the amount of change being emphathised. In using the word processor, world wide web and internet, graphing techniques, CD ROM's, video disks, among other items, teachers may need to experience two to three years of quality staff development programmes. Objectives need to be determined for pupils to achieve sequentially in using modern technology. Progress by pupils may well be slow, but sure with good teaching, in using technology to achieve objectives.

Second, staff development programmes might well be extensive if an interdisciplinary curriculum is to be evidence. An allied arts programme of instruction may well emphasise a team teaching approach. Allied arts attempts in integrate art, music, dance, drama, poetry and architecture, among other possibilities. Thus a teaching team consisting of the following teachers, each qualified in his/her area of expertise—an art, a music, a physical education, and a literature or English teacher—must be in the offing. If possible, an architecture from the community might be hired part time. If a school system has an architect, it becomes easier for this person to work on the team to plan the objectives, learning opportunities, and evaluation procedures than would otherwise be the case. Staff development programmes might then include members learning to plan together, developing means of curricular integration of content, and evaluating to ascertain the effectiveness of the teaching team. Team teaching has built in inservice education opportunities since members may learn from each other during planning sessions.

Third, cooperative learning, as activities and experiences for pupils to achieve objectives, may need staff development programmes. The goals of the staff development programme might stress how to form groups for cooperative learning, how to work effectively as a teacher with diverse groups in the classroom, and how to appraise pupil performance within a group. The classroom teacher needs to believe in cooperative learning for it to become effective in the classroom setting.

Three needs to be a caring attitude towards each other in cooperative learning endeavours. Pupils who feel neutral to each other or possess findings of hostility might well fail to become good members of a committee in cooperative learning endeavours. Noddings (1995) wrote the following:

The greatest structural obstacle, however, may be simply legitimising the inclusion of themes of care in the curriculum. Teachers in the early grades have long included such themes as a regular part of their work, and middle school educators are becoming more sensitive to developmental needs in involving care. But, secondary schools—where violence, apathy, and alienation are most evident—do little to develop the capacity to care. Today, even elementary teachers complain that the pressure to produce high test scores inhibit the work they believe is central to their mission: the development of competent and caring people. Therefore it would seem that the most fundamental change required is one of attitude. Teachers can be very special people in the lives of children, and it should be legitimate for them to spend time developing relations of trust, taking with students about problems that are central to their lives, and guiding them toward greater sensitivity and competence across all the domains of care.

Fourth, peer coaching may be used to assist teachers to hone and perfect teaching skills in any curriculum area. Two teachers working together may observe each other's teaching and discuss the quality of objectives to be stressed, the aligning of learning opportunities with the objectives, and evaluation to ascertain if the objectives have been achieved by pupils. Showers and Joyce (1996), strong advocates of peer coaching, wrote the following:

When staff development becomes the major vehicle for school improvement, schools should take into account both the structures and content of training, as well as changes needed in the workplace to make possible the collaborative planning, decision making, and data collection that are essential to organisational change efforts. As we ponder ways to ensure that learning/coaching fuels the school renewal process, we are also examining how the culture of the school can increasingly provide a benign environment for collective activity.

A cohesive school culture makes possible the collective decisions that generate schoolwide improvement efforts. The formation of peer coaching teams produces greater faculty cohesion and focus and, in turn, facilitates more skillful shared decision making. A skillful staff development programme results in a self-perpetuating process for change as well as knowledge and skills for teachers and increased learning for pupils.

Peer coaching might then be used to improve the quality of learning opportunities for pupils as well as select objectives and evaluation procedures for learners. Learning opportunities (Ediger, 1994) should emphasise that pupils experience:

1. meaningful lessons and units of study. With meaning, pupils understand and comprehend that which was contained in ongoing learning opportunities;
2. interesting content and skills in the curriculum. With interest, the pupil and the curriculum become one, not separate entities. Pupils attend and achieve from ongoing lessons and units of study;
3. purpose in learning. With purpose in learning, pupils accept reasons for attaining relevant facts, concepts, and generalisations presented...;
4. sequence in learning, with quality sequence, pupils relate newly acquired content with that previously achieved. Previous knowledge attained provides readiness of the new objectives to be achieved...;
5. balance among objectives stressed. Thus, knowledge, skills, and attitudes—three kinds of objectives need

to be achieved by students. These objectives interact and are not in isolation from each other. For example, if pupils possess positive attitudes, they should achieve needed knowledge and skills more readily.

Traditional organisation of learning opportunities stress using textbooks heavily, workbooks, work sheets, and recitation methods of instruction. A separate subjects curriculum tends to be in evidence with traditional approaches in teaching. Moving away from the separate subjects curriculum is correlation, then fusion, and finally the interdisciplinary curriculum. Skill in planning is needed to move away from the usual ways of teaching to that which harmonises more so with learner growth and development characteristics. Each pupil is to realise optimal development in knowledge, skills, and attitudes or the affective dimension. A multimedia approach is recommended in teaching to provide for individual differences.

Evaluation of Pupil Progress

Traditional procedures of evaluating pupil achievement has been to use standardised and norm referenced testing. Teacher written test items have also been used much in the past to ascertain pupil progress. These procedures are still recommended to determine pupil achievement. However, addition procedures must be used. Teacher observation needs to be used to notice learner progress in contextual situations. Thus within a given activity, the teacher notices how well each pupil is programming. Assistance is given to pupils as is necessary. Pupils might then continue to work in context on the project or activity being pursued.

A relatively recent development is for pupils with teacher guidance to develop a portfolio of achievement and progress. In the portfolio, the pupil places samples of activities completed. These include written work, art projects, snapshots of construction experiences, videotapes of dramatic endeavours, and cassette recordings of speech activities, among others. The portfolio may also contain test results, journal entries, rating scales, rubrics, and checklists to indicate learner progress and achievement. Materials for the portfolio must be carefully chosen; otherwise it may become too voluminous. Contents in the portfolio are to show interested persons accomplishments of the involved pupil. A variety of learning opportunities experienced by a learner must show its related accomplishments to others who are interested in seeing the individual pupils achievements.

Kane and Khattri (1995) wrote:

Some questions related to performance assessment remain to be answered by future research. They have to do with basic and secondary issues in educational reform. What knowledge and skills are students expected to demonstrate after a certain period of schooling? What other systematic reforms must be undertaken in order for assessment reforms to be effective? Which assessment formats are most useful for which specific purposes? The greatest challenge ahead lies in designing systems of school reform that synergistically support the core educational functions of teaching and learning for which teachers are most powerful "engine".

REFERENCES

Bloom, Benjamin S. (1956). *Taxonomy of Educational Objectives, Handbook one—Cognitive Domain*. London, England: Longmans Publishing House.

Earnest Vimala (1995). *The Relative Effectiveness of Teaching Volumetric Experiments in Chemistry using Simpson's Taxonomy of Educational Objectives for the Psychomotor Domain—An Experimental Study*, Ph.D. Thesis. University of Madras, India, pp. 4-21.

Ediger, Marlow (1988), *The Elementary Curriculum*, 2nd Edition, Kirksville, Missouri: Simpson Publishing Company, pp. 117-126.

Ediger, Marlow (1994) *"Early Field Experiences in Teacher Education"*, *College Student Journal*, 28: 302.

Fenstermacher, Gary D. (1995). "The Absence of Democratic and Educational Ideals from Contemporary Educational Reforms Initiatives", *Educational Horizons*, 73-70.

Kane, Michael B., and Nidh Khattri (1995) "Assessment reform," the *Phi Delta Kappan*, 77: 32.

Krathwohl, David, et al. (1956), *The Taxonomy of Educational Objectives—Handbook Two, Affective Domain*. London, England: Longmans Publishing House.

Noddings, Neil (1995) "Teaching themes of Care", *Phi Delta Kappan*, 76: 679.

Showers, Beverly, and Bruce Joyce (1996), "The Evolution of Peer Coaching", *Educational Leadership*, 53: 16.

17

Inservice Education and the Curriculum

Inservice education needs to be in evidence in order to improve the curriculum. Merely having diverse training programmes for staff members will not guarantee a quality curriculum for students. Definite objectives, experience to attain the chosen ends, and evaluation procedures need utilising to implement improved inservice education programmes for administrators and teachers. Unruh and Unruh wrote:

> Planning for implementation is critical in the process of curriculum improvement. Frequently, the planning process extends only as far as creating new ideas or adopting them from elsewhere, initiating a process, and developing the new or revised curriculum plan, but then it stops short or planning out the actual implementation process. Essential strategies for implementation, which may require two years or more for development, include; acquiring sufficient resources, involving the implements on a continuing basis and arranging for planned channels or two-way communication among the participants.

Faculty Meetings and Inservice Education

Numerous educators have hailed the effects of faculty meetings in the school setting to improve the curriculum. There are teachers, however, who believe that faculty meetings participated in have not been as profitable as they might have been. Ediger wrote the following emphasising quality criteria in conducting faculty meetings:

Faculty meetings in an elementary school can be used wisely in improving the social studies curriculum. Properly developed criteria need to be utilised in implementing concepts pertaining to improving the elementary school social studies programme through the use of faculty meetings.

1. Each faculty member of an elementary school should have ample opportunities to provide input in terms of the agenda to be used at a faculty meeting.
2. All faculty members should have numerous opportunities to serve on a committee to arrange problem areas for consideration on an agenda.
3. The agenda should be ready for faculty member study, approximately, two days before the meeting.
4. Faculty members should identify relevant problems to discuss at a faculty meeting. These problem areas may include changing from the use of basal social studies texts to a more individualised approach in reading content, using management systems in the teaching of social studies, and integrating science, mathematics, as well as language arts, into the social studies curriculum.
5. Participants in a faculty meeting may volunteer to serve on a committee of their own choosing to solve relevant problems. Individual study in attempting to resolve an identified problem may also become an inherent part of the faculty meeting.
6. Adequate resource materials should be available to help individuals in the area of problem solving. These resources may include college and university level textbook in the teaching of elementary school social studies, professional periodical articles in this area, as well as related films, filmstrips, tapes, slides, and resource personnel.
7. Direct teaching of pupils using innovative ideas may also become an inherent part of these faculty meetings. Tape recording and video taping of lessons

may provide participants, needed data to improve teaching-learning situations in the social studies. Faculty meetings can aid in improving the curriculum if:

1. Teachers, as well as administrators, have input into the agenda. Thus, each participants needs to participate perceive or reasons for attending faculty meetings.
2. Individual differences among members are adequately provided for. Opportunities then need to be evidence for participants individually to pursue and solve relevant problem areas.
3. Understanding, skills, and attitudinal goals achieved in the faculty meeting might be implemented in the school and classroom setting.
4. Appropriate materials and facilities are available to promote an environment conducive to learning.

Workshops and Inservice Education

There are numerous educators who extol the utilisation of workshops to improve the curriculum. Merely having a plethora of workshops does not guarantee an improved curriculum for each learner.

There is a definite philosophy that needs to be followed by involved persons pertaining to the workshop concept. Cooperation is one vital concept in developing quality workshops. Thus, administrators and teachers need to work together harmoniously in deciding upon the theme of the ensuing workshops. The theme needs to reflect such concepts as significance, purpose, as well as being worthwhile and relevant.

Cooperatively, adequate facilities and resource materials need to be decided upon by workshop participants.

Generally, three levels of participation are emphasised in workshop. The first level—the general session—involves all members of a workshop identifying problems of concern in improving the curriculum. Each person needs to participate to select problems. Teachers and administrators experience problems in the school and community environment. A good place to choose relevant problems resides in the general session.

Each workshop participant should volunteer to serve on a committee in attempting to solve a specific problem. A variety of reference materials may be utilised in the problem solving activity. Thus, reading materials, as well as slides, films, filmstrips, cassettes, and consultant help may well provide needed guidance in the problem solving situation.

To provide more adequately for individual differences, the third level of workshop concept needs implementation. Thus, each workshop participant must have ample opportunities to work on a project of his/her very own choosing. Adequate resources need to be available to assist in solving the chosen problem area. The following examples are given as possible problems to identify and solve:

1. Working with a disrupter in the classroom.
2. Guiding the gifted and talented learner.
3. Helping pupils with reading problems.
4. Using a variety of techniques to appraise pupil achievement.
5. Wanting needed innovations in the curriculum.

Wiles and Lovell wrote the following pertaining to the workshop concept to improve the quality of teaching and learning:

In the planning of a workshop, provision is made for great emphasis on evolution—of the process, the ways of working together and the learning outcomes. During the entire programme the evaluation is a continuous process in which all members of the group participate. It is unusual in most workshops to establish an evaluation committee that has the responsibility of recommending evaluation procedures to the total group and of organising and carrying out the evaluation procedures to the total group and organising and carrying out the evaluation procedures the workshop group accepts. Evaluation periods with the discussion under the leadership of a panel composed of members of the various work groups have proved to be an effective way of improving the workshop process. Almost all workshops have found it advisable to use, in addition, a formal check sheet to focus the attention of the workshop members on the important phases of the working experience and to help everyone to strengthen weak points. Workshop members grow in teaching skill through opportunities to analyse who group activities are productive or unsatisfactory.

Visiting Innovative Classrooms

Teachers and administrators may observe as well as appraise experimental teaching and learning situations by visiting specific schools. Hopefully, the end result will be to implement that which was deemed worthwhile from the innovative school.

Vital methods of teaching to be accepted and implemented must assist each pupil to progress in an optimal manner. Thus, each learner needs to achieve relevant understandings, skills, and attitudinal goals. A variety of learning activities must be provided to guide pupils to achieve objectives. Why should the concept "variety" be emphasised? Pupils have diverse learning styles. There are selected pupils who might achieve more optimally with the utilisation of reading as a major means of learning. Others might achieve at a more optimal manner with the utilisation of concrete (actual objects and items, as well as experiencing excursions) and semi-concrete (film, filmstrips, slides, transparencies, and illustration, among others) materials.

A variety of appraisal procedures need utilising to evaluate learner progress. Why? No procedure is perfect, by any means. Thus, one method of appraising is a check against other approaches. Teacher written test items (true-false, multiple choice, matching, completion, and essay) rating scales, checklists, attitudinal, inventories, standardised tests, criterion reference tests, anecdotal statements, among others, might be used to assess learner achievement.

Teachers and administrators continually need to locate improved objectives, learning activities, and appraisal procedures. Otherwise, the curriculum might remain stagnant.

Which innovations then might administrators and teachers observe and thus, hopefully improve the curriculum?

1. Team teaching, the nongraded school, and dual progress plans of grouping pupils for instruction.
2. Individualised reading, colour, coding, and diacritical marking systems in guiding pupils to read at an increased level of proficiency.
3. Implementing process objectives in the curriculum.
4. Using formative and summative distinctions in appraising the curriculum.
5. Using teaching performance tests, mastery learning, and criterion-referenced supervision.
6. Utilisation peer learning, the contract system, as well as learning centres and open space education.

Pertaining to inservice education, Rao and Drake write the following:

1. Inservice education should be directly related to a specific goal and/or objective of the educational programme.
2. Channels should be maintained so that inservice needs may be easily communicated and initiated from the faculty.
3. Tangible commitments in the form of money, time, and materials need to be made by the central administration and school board. Commitments of time and energy should also be expected from the teachers.
4. Communications with the whole system is essential to ensure participation by those interested as well

as at least partial avoidance of misinformation regarding the purpose, or cause, of the inservice programme.

5. A carefully designed evaluation of the inservice programme should be considered part of every inservice attempt. The evaluation should be directly related to the effect upon the main clients of the school—the pupils.

Using Teaching Performance Tests

There are selected educators emphasising that teachers be tested to reveal competency. Diverse approaches might be utilised here. One method, as a model, will now be described. Administrators may develop measurably stated objectives for learners to achieve. These objectives are provided to teachers, e.g., one set to be utilised in teaching a given set of pupils. The teacher is also provided background subject matter to be used in planning a lesson directly related to the measurable goals. The teacher then needs to select learning activities to guide learners in achieving the stated objectives. A sample of measurement (test items) procedures may also be provided to teachers.

The administrators needs to choose pupils who have not achieved the precise ends yet can attain the chosen objectives.

After the teacher has had ample opportunity to prepare the lesson, he/she is ready to teach it to the chosen learners. Pupils are then tested to notice if objectives have been attained. The administrator then notices which objectives have/have not been attained by learners. The success of the involved teacher depends upon the number of measurable stated objectives achieve by pupils.

Preferably, a teacher should take more than one performance test to demonstrate proficiency in teaching. Tests must be safeguarded so that they might be utilised again by other teachers in the school.

James Poham wrote the following guidelines in using teaching performance tests for instructional improvement and skills assessment:

1. Allow sufficient planning time for the teacher.
2. Use naive but teachable learners.
3. Use small or large groups of learners.
4. Item sampling post tests may be used.
5. Routinely assess learner affect.

For instructional improvement:

1. Clinical observers should conduct instructional analysis on basis of learner performance.
2. Provide opportunities for re-planning and re-teaching of unsuccessful learners.

For skill assessment:

1. All relevant conditions should be comparable for each teacher.
2. Assign learners to teachers randomly.
3. More than one performance test should be completed by each teacher.
4. Preserve test security.

Independent Studies and Inservice Education

Numerous relevant topics exist from which teachers may choose to develop an independent study involving a problem area. A topic that is chosen needs to possess purpose for the involved teacher. A solution to a vital problem in teaching and learning needs to be a significant end result. A variety of reference source, including consultant assistance, should be in the offing. An adequate amount of time must be given to compete a quality independent study.

Which areas might be relevant to pursue in an independent study? The following are given as suggestions:

1. Diagnosing learner achievement in reading.
2. Utilising science equipment proficiently.
3. Using innovative techniques to appraise pupil progress.

4. Implementing recommend procedures in reporting learner achievement to parents.
5. Emphasising affective goals in teaching and learning.
6. Emphasising computer assisted instruction.

In Conclusion

There are numerous inservice techniques available to improve the curriculum. Each administrator and teacher must work in the direction of providing quality experiences in order that pupils individually might progress optimally. Hass wrote:

In selecting goals and objectives curriculum planners make choices regarding the relative importance given to society, human development, learning and knowledge, and cognition in planning the curriculum. Philosophy enters into every curriculum decision that is made. There is rarely a moment in the school day when a teacher is not confronted with situations in which philosophy is a part of determining the choices that are made. It is one's (usually covert) answers to such questions as "What is the good person?" "What is the good society?" "What is the good life?" that determine action. All curriculum thinking and work is value based.

REFERENCES

Ediger, Marlow, *The Elementary Curriculum, A Handbook*. Kirksville, Misouri: Simpson Publishing Company, 1977, Pages 134-135.

Hass, Glen, *Curriculum Planning: A New Approach*. Newton Massachusetts: Allyn and Bacon, Inc., 1983.

Popham, James W., *Using Teaching Performance Tests for Instructional Improvement and Skill Assessment*. Log Angelos, California: Vimcet Associates, 1971 (Filmstrip and Cassette).

Roe, William H., and Drake, Thelbert L., *The Principalship*, Second Edition. New York: The Macmillan Company, 1980, Page 274.

Unruh, Glenys G., and Adolph Unruh, *Curriculum Development*, Berkeley, California: McCutchan Publishing Corporation, 1984.

Wiles, Kimball, and Lovell, John T., *Supervision for Better Schools*, Fourth Edition. Englewood Cliffs, Prentice-Hall, Inc., 1975, Page 114.

18

Grouping Pupils in the Elementary School

Numerous approaches have been recommended by educators in grouping pupils for instruction. Certainly does not exist as to which plan of grouping is best. Each recommended approach of grouping pupils seemingly contains strengths as well as weaknesses. Teachers, principles, supervisors, and parents must consider and assess each of these approaches in grouping pupils for instruction. The psychology of learning is important as well as child growth and development characteristics when making a final decision pertaining to grouping pupils for instruction.

Faculty members of an elementary school need to become thoroughly knowledgeable as to the various possibilities that exist in grouping pupils for instruction. Each plan should be evaluated in terms of acceptable criteria of standards. No thinking persons would advocate new approaches to grouping without being fully knowledgeable about their strengths and weaknesses. It is important that there be widespread acceptance of a new plan for grouping before it is implemented. Teachers, principals, supervisors, and parents should be in much agreement about a new plan for grouping before it is implemented. Each elementary school should also study thoroughly the present plan being used for grouping pupils for instruction. Thus, a gap may be noticed between where the school is presently in the area of grouping pupils for instruction as compared to where it should be.

One of the most difficult tasks involved in implementing a new plan for grouping pupils may well be to get parental acceptance. Parents can be satisfied with the most traditional plan of grouping available. The lay public then must reach a stage of disequilibrium whereby they no longer are satisfied with the status quo. The following approaches may be utilised to develop this state of disequilibrium within the lay public:

1. Talks given at Parent-Teacher Association meetings pertaining to new plans of grouping pupils for instruction.
2. Ideas about new plans for grouping being injected when parent-teacher conferences are held.
3. Newspaper articles bringing in terms pertaining to new approaches in grouping pupils for instructional purposes.
4. The possibilities of presenting concepts and generalisation pertaining to grouping pupils on a local television or radio station should be explored.
5. Talking informally to parents at open house and on other occasions about grouping pupils for instruction.
6. Faculty members of an elementary school should discuss creative approaches in informing the lay public relating to proposed innovations in the schools.

Any plan for grouping pupils is not a panacea. It is a means to an end but not an end in and of itself. The new plan of grouping pupils for instruction should aid in improving the curriculum. It should guide in improving teaching-learning situations in the elementary school. Too frequently faculty members have felt that a new plan for grouping pupils should solve all ills in an elementary school. A newly implemented plan for grouping pupils could present many new problems to the involved school. If a team of teachers cannot work together cooperatively, the innovation may cause more grief than improvement over previous plans of grouping. An another example, in a departmentalised plan for grouping pupils, learners may not develop well emotionally and socially if the teacher goes overboard for teaching subject matter only. Intellectual development of pupils to be sure is important; however equally important is physical, social and emotional development.

Plans for grouping pupils have been misunderstood by teachers, principals, and supervisors. For example, there are elementary schools which are called "nongraded schools" by name only. Teachers by example in their teaching may be emphasising the use of fifth grade materials, for example, in teaching all fifth graders regardless of capacity and achievement levels. The nongraded philosophy is definitely not being implemented in cases such as these. "Turn teaching" has been confused with team teaching. In turn teaching, each teacher does his or her own preparing for teaching with no cooperative endeavours involved in planning together with other team members in terms of objectives, learning activities, and evaluation techniques. Each teacher then takes his turn in teaching in large group sessions as well as working with smaller groups, and involved pupils. As will be discussed later, team teaching emphasises that members of a team plan together teaching strategies for a given set of learners. It is important that teachers, principles, and supervisors understand the basic underlying principles that each plan emphasised in grouping pupils for instruction.

There will, no doubt, be different, interpretations for the philosophy or rationale behind each plan for placing pupils into groups; however, there will be considerable agreement also in interpretation of the underlying principles pertaining to each plan of grouping. For example, the nongraded elementary school states the importance of pupils experiencing continuous progress. Hardly could pupils experience continuous progress if all pupils in a class are on the same page at the same time when utilising the basal reader, for example, as a learing activity. The only exception to this case could pertain to a class of pupils which are highly homogeneous in terms of reading achievement. This would indeed be rare, however, when thirty pupils, for example, would make up the total number in a class setting. Even then there would be individual differences that need to be provided for.

The Nongraded School

The nongraded elementary school has much to offer in terms of helping learners to be successful. As was stated previously, a basic principle underlying this approach to grouping is that pupils should experience continuous progress. Teachers can be "overly ambitious" in wanting learners to achieve thus causing pupils to lost out in the ongoing activities. It is no wonder then that pupils experience failure and eventually develop or maintain feelings of inadequacy. Pupils should feel that they are achieving to their optimum thus feelings of success become a part of the child.

In the nongraded elementary school, it is important that teachers attempt to determine reading levels of pupils as early as possible. Pupils are generally grouped homogeneously based on reading achievement. It is good if an elementary school has at least three roomfuls of pupils a given chronological age. If there were only two roomfuls of eight year olds, for example, it would be difficult to group them homogeneously. The range of achievement in reading in each room would be great indeed. With three roomfuls of pupils of a given chronological age, the chances are fairly good of achieving some degree of homogeneity in grouping pupils for instruction within each classroom. More homogeneity would be possible in grouping if there were more than three roomfuls of pupils on a given age level. Within each classroom pupils could be further grouped into three different achievements levels in reading. Pupils should be placed in the reading group which is in a harmony with their level of achievement. Flexible grouping is important. It is important to put pupils in another group if they demonstrate that the original group they were placed in was not in harmony with their present achievement level. Teachers must evaluate pupil achievement continuously to determine the group that each child would benefit most from. At the end of a specific school year, the teachers should record where learners left off in terms of materials used and skills mastered. This would be important so that pupils do nor repeat unnecessarily previous materials read and skills mastered. With the beginning of a new school year, the teacher would need to do some reviewing of what learners had learned previously since some forgetting, of course, will have occurred of previously developed learnings. The teacher would also need to engage in reteaching that which necessitates doing this.

The sky is the limit in pupil achievement in the nongraded school as long as there is continuous progress for learners and success is in evidence. Thus, for example, pupils who would be in the sixth year beyond kindergarten of the nongraded schools could be reading from and using seventh and eighth grade materials providing this harmonises with their capabilities presently in reading. A slower group of pupils in the same age group may be reading from and using fourth grade reading materials since this harmonises with their present achievement level. The teacher would accept pupils where they are presently in reading achievement and help them in progress continuously.

Ideally, there should be no failures in the nongraded school. No one, of course, basically likes to be a failure or have feelings of failure. In the graded school concept, some pupils have repeated a grade since they did not achieve up to grade level in reading achievement or did not realise standards set by the teacher. Some cannot achieve up to grade level standards since they lack the necessary capacity, interest, motivation, or home background. For others, it is not challenging enough to realise fifth grade standards in reading, for example, if they are in the fifth grade. Their capacities, interests, and motivation would demand realising a higher level of achievement than the grade level they are in presently. The nongraded school emphasises the importance of providing for individual differences. If pupils fail in the graded school, they may use the same materials over again for the next school year. Certainly, this does not help learners to achieve continuous progress. He may even have the same teacher again which constantly can remind him of failure! These examples do not exemplify basic underlying principles of the nongraded school.

There are, or course, some weaknesses of the nongraded school. If pupils would be grouped homogeneously continuously, there would be no opportunities within the school setting for pupils to interact with other children of different capacity and achievement levels. Certainly life in society does not operate that way. Individuals interact with others of different capacities, interests, achievement levels, and background knowledge.

There are teachers who may not wish to teach the slowest group of pupils. They may not have the knowledge, patience, interest, and poise to work with the slowest group of achievers. The attitudes and feelings of the teacher, no doubt will be reflected within learners. To make matters worse, parents may not have the necessary positive attitudes to accept the fact that their child is in the slowest group. Certainly parental attitudes will also be reflected within their children. Parents in the home reveal their feelings toward school to their children. Sometimes, parents speak openly about their feelings toward school in front of their children. And even if words are not used in communicating feelings and attitudes, the child in the home or school generally is able to understand non-verbal communication.

It should also be pointed out that pupils grouped among the top achievers could develop negative attitudes towards those who achieve less well and have less capacity. In the class setting, teachers need to guide pupils in accepting and respecting others. Respect for others is the heart of democratic thinking.

The Self-Contained Class

Too often, educators have been prone to criticise heavily the more traditional approaches to grouping pupils for instruction, such as the self-contained classroom. Tradition does not in and of itself make a concept or idea bad. There are many traditions in life, which, no doubt, will remain with us forever. However, many customs, beliefs, values, and ideals change due to living in a changing society. Respecting others in the, home, school, and community will always be an important ideal to strive toward. Critical thinking, creative thinking, and problem solving, no doubt, also will always remain important skills for individuals to develop.

The self-contained classroom concept is based on the idea that a teacher can get to know pupils well by teaching them for the major part of the school day. Music, art, and physical education could be taught by special teachers. By knowing children well, the teacher should be able to do a good job of providing for individual differences. The teacher can get to know well the child's interests, needs, and abilities in a self-contained class. Teachers have numerous opportunities to become thoroughly familiar with the home background of each child in a self-contained classroom.

A further advantage of the self-contained class is that teachers can help pupils sense the relationship of knowledge. The teacher, for example, can guide learners to sense that social studies and science are related. In units on air, land, noise and water pollution, the teacher can guide learners in understanding basic scientific principles and generalisations pertaining to this problem in society. Children could also study the effect that pollution has on man. Thus science and social studies would be emphasised as being related. When a committee of pupils reports findings to the class pertaining to research conducted on pollution, the language arts area of speaking is involved. Thus, a teacher in a self-contained class has many opportunities to guide learners in relating knowledge so that it is not conceived to be in isolation. Too frequently, pupils have felt and thought that knowledge is compartmentalised and cannot be related. In problem solving, knowledge which is related will be used in arriving at solutions. In daily living, it is important to be able to solve problems. Solutions to these problems generally require content which is related. Too often, individuals who compartmentalise knowledge have a difficult time in using what has been learned in the process of problem solving.

Disadvantages of the self-contained classroom can also be listed. A teacher may find it difficult to teach the different curriculum areas well in a self-contained classroom. Can a teacher do justice in teaching reading and the language arts, social studies, science, mathematics and perhaps, art and physical education? It certainly does require keeping up with the many separate areas that make up the elementary school curriculum. Sometimes a teacher will say that he does not like to teach science or he does not feel competent in teaching science. That curriculum area then may be slighted and minimised by the teacher. There has been a trend in some elementary schools to departmentalise selected curriculum areas on the intermediate grade level. A teacher who has a strong background of course work in science and elementary education could then teach science to several classrooms of pupils. Other teachers could then select curriculum areas to teach in which they have a strong background of course work on the college and/or university level. Teachers should teach the curriculum area or areas in which they have the strongest background knowledge in content as well as in methodology. Elementary school pupils in many cases are aware of strengths and weaknesses that teachers have. It takes good teachers to help pupils achieve to their optimum. Subject matter knowledge of teachers, of course, is not the only important consideration or important factor in teaching. The teacher must like children and have an inward desire in wanting them to achieve to their optimum. The good teacher is respectful of children and shows the necessary patience in working with all learners so they can feel successful in learning.

The self-contained classroom then has its strengths and weaknesses as do all plans in grouping pupils for instruction. Since the self-contained room is a traditional plan for grouping, it has come under considerable criticism. However, one must realise that this plan emphasises that the teacher should now pupils well by being with a given class for a major part of a school day. Pupils in this plan for grouping can be assisted in relating knowledge. The time allotted to each curriculum area in the self-contained room can be flexible. If the teacher needs more time for teaching mathematics in a given school day, perhaps it is feasible to shorten the time devoted to teaching social studies. On a different day, needed additional time can be given for the teaching of elementary school social studies. In other words in the self-contained classroom, flexibility in scheduling different curriculum areas of the elementary school is possible.

Departmentalisation

Departmentalisation emphasises the importance of teachers being well prepared to teach in their area of areas of specialty. Thus, an elementary school teacher, for example, may teach only mathematics or only reading. The teacher in a departmentalised elementary school generally has a strong background of course work in the area he is teaching. For example, a social studies teacher will have much course work in the social sciences together with ample course work in elementary education. The student may have a double major in the two areas previously mentioned, or have a major in elementary education with a minor or an area of concentration in the social sciences. Thus, the teacher should be well prepared in terms of credit hours in a given academic area on the college and/or university level to teach in a departmentalised school. This teacher would generally have fewer daily preparations to make in a departmentalised plan as compared to the self-contained classroom. The teacher in a departmentalised school may teach social studies, for example, to five fifth or sixth grade classes.

Not many elementary schools emphasise departmentalisation on the primary grade levels. The subject matter knowledge needed on these grade levels is generally not a major problem; however, it is very important for these teachers to be warm, friendly, understanding, and help each child realise his optimum potential.

It becomes difficult to correlate or integrate different curriculum areas in the elementary school when departmentalisation is emphasised strongly. Each curriculum area may become an isolated domain unto itself. Various curriculum areas can be correlated or integrated in a departmentalised plan of grouping if teachers teaching the separate academic areas plan together. They could plan together how science and social studies may be correlated so that pupils sense degrees of relationship between these two curriculum areas. For example, when fifth grade pupils would be studying a unit on the "Age of Discovery" in social studies, they could also be developing science principles and generalisations pertaining to magnetism in a unit on "Magnetism and Electricity." With the use of steel needles and a magnet, pupils could develop resultant magnets by stroking the needles in one direction on the magnet. The magnetized needle could then be placed on a cork which is floating in a pan of water. Pupils could observe the poles of the magnetized needle. Understandings could be developed by learners pertaining to like poles of magnets repel whereas unlike poles attract. The magnetized needle would behave in a similar way in relationship to the north and south magnetic field on the surface of the earth. Compasses became important for sailors during the "Age of Discovery" when new lands and water routes were being explored and discovered.

As a further example, reading and social studies could be correlated in a departmentalised plan of grouping pupils if teachers from these two curriculum areas would plan together. If pupils are studying a unit on "Colonization in the New World" in social studies, the basal reader may have selected stories that relate to that period of time. Thus pupils would have additional opportunities to learn more about the colonists in Colonial America in the curriculum area of reading and this could be correlated with the related ongoing social studies unit. Ample time would need to be given by teachers for planning from the different curriculum areas being taught in a departmentalised plan of grouping so that subject matter areas or different academic disciples may become related in the thinking of pupils. Correlation for the sake of correlating is to be frowned upon. Correlating and integrating of content are important when it helps pupils to develop interest, purpose, and motivation for learning. Also, pupils should not think in terms of isolated, fragmented knowledge to the point of memorising unimportant facts for test purposes or under threat from teachers and parents. An excessive number of isolated facts which are learned by pupils make retention of learning a major problem. Generally, pupils will retain learnings longer if knowledge is perceived as being related rather than as isolated, unrelated bits of information.

Homogeneous Versus Heterogeneous Grouping

Educators have long debated and discussed the pros and cons of homogeneous versus heterogeneous grouping of pupils. Some have stated that homogeneous grouping is not as democratic as it could be since pupils of a similar level of achievement would be placed in a specific group. For example, the top achievers in mathematics in the sixth grade would be in one room in an elementary school followed by the second best achievers being in a different room. Other levels of mathematics achievement would be in separate rooms with the slowest learners in this curriculum area being grouped in a room by themselves. It has been felt by some educators that pupils need to interact with others regardless of achievement levels. Principals, supervisors, and teachers could provide situations whereby learners work and play together with others regardless of capacity and achievement levels even though homogeneous grouping is emphasised for several curriculum areas. For example, pupils could be grouped heterogeneously in physical education, music and art. This type of plan for grouping pupils emphasises heterogeneity in several curriculum areas of the elementary school. For other curriculum areas, homogeneous grouping could be emphasised such as in mathematics, the language arts, social studies, and science.

Teachers may find it easier to teach a given group of learners if homogeneous grouping is in evidence as compared to heterogeneous grouping since the range of achievement will not be as great within a class. However, teachers may not like to teach a class of slow learners as well as those who achieve at a faster rate of speed. The attitude of the teacher, of course, may be reflected within learners. Since the range of achievement in a class may be very great in heterogenous grouping, it may pose a problem for some teacher in providing for individual differences. In certain methods of teaching it may not matter much if heterogeneous of homogeneous grouping is utilised. For example, in individualised reading, each pupils basically select his own library book to read. He generally selects a book which is on his reading level. His own reading of the library book will involve a pace which should be in harmony with being able to comprehend the contents adequately. Each pupil in a class will read at a different rate of speed. Also each learner will select a library book which differs in complexity from other library books selected for reading by other children in the classroom. Thus, individual differences can be provided for regardless of capacity and achievement levels of pupils in a class or group. Following the reading of a library book, the teacher may have a conference with the pupil. The teacher can then get data on the learner having comprehend the contents of the library book as well as evaluating pupil interest, enthusiasm, and purpose for reading the book. The teacher can also evaluate the quality of oral reading of the child when the latter reads a section of the library book orally. The teacher can record the results of the conference for future reference. Comparisons can be made of conferences held with each pupil from one time to the next to notice changes in behaviour.

In using individualised reading in the classroom, it is obvious that heterogeneous or homogeneous grouping would not be a major problem. It becomes more of a problem when utilising basal readers if the teacher feels that all learners in a class or in a group should be at the same place at the same time in using a specific series of these readers. It is only common knowledge that learners in a class differ in capacity, achievement, interest, and motivation. Thus, learners in a class cannot be held to the same achievement without detrimental results. For some pupils the expected uniform standards of achievement of traditional teachers will be too difficult where frustration and failure may be the end result. For other learners these standards may be excessively low resulting in boredom and a lack of enthusiasm. The teacher must provide for individual differences regardless of the plan of grouping.

Team Teaching in the Elementary School

A rather recent innovation in grouping pupils for instruction is team teaching. The term "team" implies that teachers work together cooperatively in determining objectives, learning activities, and evaluation techniques when teaching a specific set of learners. Team teaching needs to be differentiated from "turn teaching". In turn teaching, each teacher does his own planning for teaching and then takes his turn teaching pupils either in a large group or small group sessions. Other teachers also take their turn teaching these learners. However, there is little or no interaction among teachers when planning the objectives, learning activities, and evaluation techniques.

Democratic planning is very important when team members work together. Team teaching emphasises that members learn from each other in planning sessions. Thus, inservice education is an inherent part of team teaching as a plan in grouping pupils for instruction. If a leader or member of a teaching team would be very domineering or autocratic, the chances are that individuals, of course, would not learn from each other. There needs to be mutual respect of personalities and ideas presented when team members select the best objectives, the best learning activities, and the best evaluation techniques to be utilised in teaching a given set of learners.

The talents of each teacher should be utilised when providing learning activities for pupils. For example, when large group instruction is utilised in teaching ninety pupils, each team member's strengths should be analysed to determine who should do the teaching in the large group session. If pupils are studying a unit on "New England-Past and Present," a team member may have travelled extensively in this area as well as studied its past history thoroughly. This team member may have excellent slides, pictures, filmstrips, and booklets pertaining to the New England area. Thus, large group instruction, no doubt, would heavily involve using the talents of this member of the team. At other times, different members of the team will be utilising their talents involving large group instruction in team teaching.

After the large group session has been completed, all teachers on the team should guide learners in small group sessions. Here, learners can ask questions pertaining to the content of learning activities presented in large group instruction. Additional learning activities, carefully selected, can be provided in small group sessions. The teacher needs to select activities which are meaningful, interesting and purposeful to learners. Pupils need to be actively involved in ongoing learning activities. A variety of learning activities should be provided for learners in small group sessions. It should be pointed out that in large group instruction, the teaching team must consider and select those learning activities which capture pupil curiosity and are relevant for learners. If activities are not selected carefully, it will be difficult to hold the attention of pupils and valuable time in learning will be lost.

Ample opportunity also needs to be given to pupils to work on individual projects and activities. With the guidance of the teaching team, pupils should work on purposeful projects and activities on an individual basis which relate to the large and small group sessions.

Team teaching has long emphasised the importance of teachers using their time wisely in what they were trained and educated to do. Thus, teachers should teach and plan for teaching rather than performing routine tasks such as collecting lunch and milk money, putting overshoes of pupils, and keeping attendance records. During the school day, there should be time available for planning. Planning should not be done before the school day begins and after it ends only. In team approach, some planning can, of course, be done, during the school day. For example, a team which teaches only social studies in a school year should have a free period each school day when planning can be done.

There are numerous plans available which emphasis basic principles related to team teaching. In the master teacher plan, a teacher would be designated as the leader of the team with status difference. This individual may also receive more salary than other team members due to having additional responsibilities. The master teacher should have demonstrated teaching proficiency in the curriculum area or areas his team is responsible for. His background of course work on the college and/or university level should be strong relating again to the curriculum area or areas his team assumes responsibility for. The master teacher would then be the leader of the team when planning sessions are conducted. He should be able to work together well with others, particularly, team members. The team approach in planning sessions involves "give" and "take" as far as verbal interaction is concerned. The group rather than the individual determines objectives, learning activities, and evaluation techniques.

Another plan for implementing ideas pertaining to team teaching would involve a team of teachers with no one individual being designated as the leader. Teacher A, for example, would present an idea. This idea could be modified by other team members. Teacher B then could modify, substantiate, or bring in new ideas in the planning session. Each teacher as he or she participates becomes the leader at the time ideas are being presented. In planning sessions, the best of thinking must be emphasised. Each idea must be assessed in terms of its worth and value rather than on who presented the idea or ideas. Selected teachers may feel uncomfortable when their ideas are being evaluated by other teachers in a planning session. A teacher may also feel uncomfortable when teaching in front of other teachers in large group sessions. In other words, team teaching may not be the best approach to use in grouping pupils for instruction as far as all elementary school teachers are concerned. Some teachers, of course, will do a better job of teaching in a self-contained classroom where there is little interaction with other teachers in the school pertaining to actual teaching-learning situations. Team teaching, however, can be very beneficial to many classroom teachers. Team members can learn much from each other in planning sessions if a democratic atmosphere exists. Some teachers are motivated to do a better job of teaching if other teachers are observing them in large group or small group sessions as well as when helping pupils in individual projects. Teachers on teams need to be flexible in their thinking so that ideas can be modified and the best of thinking is then in evidence pertaining to teaching-learning situations. When ideas are constructively criticised in planning sessions, teachers should not be offended at these suggestions. Rather, teachers should perceive this situation as occasions to improve the quality of teaching. Inservice education then becomes a part of the planning sessions.

Grouping within a Class

To provide for individual differences, pupils should have ample opportunities to work in groups. There should be ample times when pupils may select the group they wish to work in. For example, pupils in a class are studying a unit pertaining to Australia. A committee of pupils could be making a relief map of that country. A second committee may be developing a model sheep and cattle station, while a third committee is gathering information from several sources for a report on manufacturing in Australia. Perhaps, a fourth committee would be involved in dramatising situations relating to wheat farming in Australia. In teacher-pupil planning sessions, cooperative decisions can be made pertaining to the goals each committee is to realise. Ultimately, each pupil can select the committee he would want to participate in.

There will be times when the teacher may appoint individual pupils to work on different committees. In the example given previously pertaining to committee work in a unit on Australia, the teacher could select pupils to work on each of the committees. For example, pupils who do well in reading content may be placed on the committee doing research on manufacturing in Australia. Other pupils having good eye-hand coordination may be appointed to serve on the committee making the relief map on Australia. In other words, the teacher is placing pupils in committees based on learner capacity, achievement, and interest. All pupils should achieve relevant understanding, skills, and attitudes.

The teacher could use the sociometric device to determine committee members. In using this device to evaluate social and personal growth, the teacher could ask questions of pupils pertaining to the following two areas:

1. If you were doing research on Australia, who would be your first, second, and third choice in selecting committee members to work with you?
2. If you were making a relief map or dramatising a scene relating to Australia, who would be your first choice, second choice, and third choice, in terms of committee members?

The questions need to be worked on the understanding level of pupils. Pupils must feel confident that the teacher will keep the information obtained strictly confidential. The teacher can use the data to determine committee members. Certainly, pupils will do better work in committees if they can get along well with each other as compared to having a lack of harmony. To be sure, a few learners may feel that being on a committee with friends provides situations where "goofing-off" or "having a picnic" is in order. The teacher needs to develop standards or criteria with pupils when emphasising committee work so that optimum achievement for all will be in evidence.

It can be excellent if interage grouping is emphasised in the elementary school. In society people of different ages interact with others regardless of age levels. Thus, pupils in an elementary school should have ample opportunities to play and work together regardless of age levels.

Having completed the relief map, the research, the model sheep and cattle station, and having practiced dramatisations pertaining to Australia, pupils from other classes of different age levels can be invited to the classroom to observe the ending or culminating of the social studies unit "Living in Australia". In situations such as these, pupils who are visiting the class which is ending a unit on Australia can learn much content as well as methodology in teaching. Perhaps, the visitors may wish to have similar learning activities in their own classroom. When teachers have ample opportunities to view the teaching procedures used by other professionals, the quality of teaching in many cases should improve.

Criteria for Grouping Pupils

Each elementary should critically evaluate and develop criteria pertaining to grouping pupils for instruction. Criteria that are developed should harmonise with research findings on child growth and development characteristics. The type or plan of grouping that is implemented in the elementary school should help pupils to achieve to their optimum in intellectual, physical, social and emotional development. The following questions should be considered when evaluating different plans in grouping pupils for instruction:

1. Does the plan of grouping pupils aid in providing for individual differences within a specific class?
2. Does the plan provide ample opportunities for pupils to engage in committee work?
3. Would pupils achieve agreed upon objectives most effectively when this plan of grouping is used?
4. Do teachers think and feel that the plan for grouping being considered would assist them in doing the best job of teaching?
5. Does the plan for grouping pupils for instruction harmonise with the architecture of the school?
6. Does the elementary school have ample audio-visual aids and other materials for teaching which would harmonise with the plan being considered in grouping pupils for instruction?
7. Do parents and the lay public adequately understand and accept the new plan for grouping before it is implemented?
8. Would the plan harmonise with revised, up-to-date educational objectives of the local elementary school?
9. Would the plan in grouping pupils for instruction harmonise with what is known about child growth and development characteristics?
10. Would the plan harmonise with the concepts and generalisations of a democracy?
11. Could a teacher learn from other professionals in the elementary school when a specific plan of grouping pupils for instruction is utilised?
12. Do pupils have ample opportunities to interact with learners of different capacity and achievement levels as well as with those of similar capacity and achievement?
13. Would pupils have occasions to work with learners of a younger age level as well as with older children?

14. Would the plan of grouping pupils for instruction provide the child with needed security and status?

Numerous plans exist in grouping pupils for instruction. Each plan has its strength and weaknesses. Thus, careful evaluation of each plan is important before it is implemented. The nongraded elementary school places primary emphasis upon continuous progress of learners. The self-contained classroom stresses the importance of teachers getting to know pupils well so that this information can be used to do a better job of teaching. Relating of different curriculum areas is also emphasised as being important in the self-contained classroom. The departmentalised elementary school emphasises the importance of having pupils in a class who are as alike as possible in capacity and achievement. Heterogeneous grouping emphasises the importance of learners having a variety of capacity and achievement levels within a specific class. In team teaching, teacher strengths must be utilised in teaching a specific curriculum area, such as social studies, science, mathematics, or reading. This would be true of large group and small group sessions as well as in aiding learners in individual study. In a team approach, members have ample opportunities to learn from each other when planning sessions are in operation to determine objectives, learning activities, and evaluation techniques for a given set of learners. Teachers in a team approach have occasions to observe each other in teaching-learning situations. Within a class setting, the teacher must use a variety of acceptable criteria in grouping pupils for instruction in order to provide for individual differences.

19

Fundamentalism Versus the Public Schools

Fundamentalism here is defined as ideas and beliefs as to what the goals in public school education should be. Selected electronic ministers as fundamentalists are able to secure much money from givers to support their ideas and beliefs in a rather vocal way. Time purchased on radio and television in particular, has had its impact in the United States.

Each fundamentalist proclaims the Bible as the voice of God. It has an enticing appeal when a fundamentalist minister holds up a copy of The Bible and states that the philosophy of the founding fathers was based on literal interpretation of Biblical content. Each minister seemingly proclaims to not interpret but tell the audience exactly what is in the Bible as it is written, in and of itself. The fundamentalist minister claims that literal, not figurative interpretations is emphasised.

After a brief introduction of how holy the Bible is, the fundamentalist pursues topics of nationalism and ethnocentrism. To the writer, it appears that little is mentioned of content in the Bible. The Bible, rather, becomes a rallying cry for the fundamentalist minister in terms of the kind of society, he would like to have in the United States. This kind of society may have quite different rules, laws, and regulations as are presently in evidence in these United States.

Fundamentalist ministers then advocate:

1. Religious instruction and prayer in the public schools. The fundamentalist minister states that public schools Godless and atheistic. However, in the United States, pluralism in religious beliefs is strongly in evidence. No mention is made by these fundamentalists of providing for religious beliefs of devout Moslems, Jews and Buddhists, among others.
2. Secular humanism being stressed in public schools. It is not clear what secular humanism is other than God is "left out" of the public schools.
3. Strong emphasis upon the free enterprises system. The Bible makes zero statements about advocating the economic system presently in evidence in the United States. Fundamentalists interpret the free enterprise systems in terms of what exists today in the United States. There, of course, are numerous grants, subsidies, and other forms of governmental aid in the economic system of the United States today.
4. Heavy defense spending. Huge weapons systems are a part of the rapidly increasing defense budget. The MX missile, star wars research, nerve gas, the Bl bomber, among other expenditures for the military, has made defense spending a high priority. Spending governmental money domestically is viewed as helping people who are not worthy. The "welfare cheats" is a target of fundamentalist ministers.
5. Creationism taught to be taught in the public schools. Evolution is perceived as an evil in which "man descended from monkeys." There of course are ministers and priests who perceive no problems in harmonising evolution with teachings of Christianity. These religious leaders might say that God created in the past and continually creates. The great educator Friedrich Froebel (1782-1852), son of a minister, took a similar point of view that God is always creating. God did not create in the Beginning only, but he also creates presently. Thus, Froebel

believed that since God was creative in creating, thus pupils should also emphasise creativeness in the school curriculum.

Fundamentalist ministers believe there are absolutes that all should adhere to. The absolutes are not to be questioned, discussed, and analysed. Generally, these rigid standards adhere to what fundamentalist ministers would like to see in their ideal state. This ideal state, no doubt, would differ much from what is presently true in the United States. The ideal may have little relationship to what is stated in the Bible. The Bible is more of a rallying cry and a symbol of conservatism pertaining to the New Right.

6. A three r's (reading, writing and arithmetic curriculum). Other academic areas, particularly, music, art, physical education, and values clarification would be minimised or omitted. Art, music, and physical education might be labelled as frills and fads. Values clarification would be taboo, according to fundamentalist ministers. Higher levels of thinking, such as problem solving, analysing, synthesising and evaluating would not be emphasised. Students, no doubt, should refrain from appraising foreign policy, deeds, and acts of the United States. Nor should the pros and deeds of enemy nations be recognised. The concept of *hate* toward enemy nations would be strongly emphasised.

Biblical Statements on Prayer

There is little if any relationship, between what the Bible states and fundamentalist philosophy. Group vocal prayer lead by a teacher does not harmonise with Biblical teaching. Instead of group prescribed prayer, the Sermon on the Mount (Matthew 6: 5-6) reads as follows:

1. And when thou prayest, thou shalt not be as the hypocrities are; for they love to pray standing in the synagogues and in the corners of the streets, that they may be seen of men. Verily I say unto you, they have their reward.

2. But thou, when thou prayest, enter into thy closet and when thou hast shut thy door, pray to thy father which is in secret; and thy father which seeth in secret shall reward thee openly.

Thus, prayer need to be given privately without the attention of others in the classrooms. Praying in secret is emphasised in the Bible. In the public school classroom, a pupil may pray anytime he/she wishes. Prayer seems to be a personal matter and indicates it is private. Freedom of the right to pray or not to pray has always been the perogative of each pupil in the public schools. No one else need know if a student, teacher, supervisor or principal is praying.

It truly cannot be said that secular humanism or God is left out of the public schools is the rule in the public schools. Religious beliefs are personal to the involved person and cannot be measured. Religion and its ideals are inherent in the conscience of the individual. To the degree that conscience is used in making moral decisions denies precise measurement. In *general* what is inherent in the conscience may be observed or inferred, in degrees.

Biblical Statements on the Free Enterprise System

In the United States, much emphasis is placed upon the private sector representing the ideal system of economics. The private sector involves individuals, groups, and corporations establishing businesses in their diverse forms. Opposite of the private sector is the public sector. The latter emphasises governmental assistance in terms of food stamps, aid to families with dependent children (AFDP) aid to farmers, as well as businesses and corporations. The public sector is advertised as making for inefficiency, red tape, waste, and promoting habits of indifference to work with food stamps and AFDP. Farmers over the decades have received governmental assistance projects such as seeding grassed waters and other conservation of soil programmes, as well as retiring land from production with payments involved for participants. Chrysler Corporation, a few years ago, received governmental loans in order to survive a recession in car sales. Southern senators and representatives have been successful in securing governmental subsidies for farmers growing tobacco.

Strong advocates of the private sector and the free enterprise system, as it presently operates in the United States, stress the ideals of capitalism even though they like governmental aid for their personal interests in the economic world.

John Calvin (1509-1564), Protestant leader in Geneva, Switzerland, advocated hard work, thrift, as well as early to bed and early to rise beliefs. Gambling and drinking were banned. Prostitutes were rounded up and reeducated. Calvin believed strongly in capitalism. In many ways, John Calivin's philosophy is strongly admired. However, unemployment due to automation, ill health, accidents, factory as well as business closures and misfortunes in general hinder people from achieving John Calvin's goals. However, little if anything is said in the Bible pertaining to Calvin's economic system.

There is a Mennonite sect living in South Dakota, North Dakota, Montana, and Washington state, known as the Hutterites. The Hutterites had their beginning in Czechoslovakia in 1528. Since that time, a central theme in their philosophical beliefs is communal ownership of property, not individual ownership. Biblical beliefs supporting collectivism are contained in Acts 4: 32-37:

32. And the multitude of them that believed were of one heart and of one soul: neither said any of them that ought of the things which he possessed was his own; but thy had all things common.

33. And with great power gave the apostles witness of the resurrection of the Lord Jesus: and great grace was upon them all.

34. Neither was there any among them that lacked: for as many as were possessors of lands or houses sold them, and brought the prices of the things that were sold.

35. And laid them down at the apostles' feet: and distribution was made unto every man according as he had need.
36. And Joses, who by the apostles was surnamed Barnabas, (which is, being interpreted, The son of consolation) a Levite, and of the country of Cyprus.
37. Having land, sold it, and brought the money, and laid it at the apostles' feet.

Paul Gross, a Hutterite wrote the following to emphasise communal ownership of property inherent in literal interpretation of the Bible:

The spirit that rules is common to all. It cannot show a lack of concern under any circumstances. On the other hand, if a responsible member turns sick during the night or is otherwise unable to discharge his duties, he does not need to worry at all, as other members can step into place at once, even if they are taken from some other department. Some positions could not be left vacant even for a day, lest the whole colony be affected. In such circumstances no selfish desire or jealousy can reign in any heart, for this would undermine the organic whole. Brotherly love and the uniting spirit of working together help to make the commune function. To an extent, salvation is expected from work, for the spirit of brotherly labour is free from all selfish desires and motives. As all the members are brought up together from childhood in such an environment and atmosphere, it creates in their minds the assurance that whatever they do for their fellows is in reality also done for themselves. Thus they find joy in their creative labour from which they profit. Here no labourer works for a landlord, but every man works for his fellow and for himself, and as the labour is shared, so also are the fruits of it divided unto every man according to his need.

The Hutterites definitely emphasise practicing what is written in the Bible. Figurative or sybolic interpretation is frowned upon. The Hutterites have concluded that to be a Christian, one must be a member of a bruderhof or commune. Sharing of goods is central to their way of living. At an early age, a child is taught to work for the good of the bruderhof and not for the self. Individual ownership of property would be considered evil or sinful. The young child is selfish and must learn the Hutterite way. The Hutterite way is to follow Acts 4: 32-37.

Laziness, indifference, carelessness in work performed are definitely not a goal of the Hutterites. Purpose and reason are involved in decisions made.

The writer has attempted to indicate that the fundamentalist would have a weak footing to say that the Bible emphasises the free enterprise system of economics. Why? Biblical content emphasises caring for the needy, sharing with others and being concerned about people (Matthew 5: 40-42):

40. And if any man will sue thee at the law, and take away thy coat, let him have thy cloak also.
41. And whosoever shall compel thee to go a mile, go with him twain.
42. Give to him the asketh thee, and from him that would borrow of thee turn not thu away.

Matthew 6: 19-21

19. Lay not up for yourselves treasures upon earth, where moth and rust doth corrupt, and where thieves break through and steal.
20. But lay up for yourselves treasures in heaven, where neither moth nor rust doth corrupt, and where thieves do not break through nor steal.
21. For where your treasure is, there will your heart be also.

In Hutterite society, old people, the ill and the retarded are taken care of on the commune. Any person in need has needs taken care of.

The writer has had rather perfect health for fifty seven years. Seemingly, he functions rather well in the free enterprise system, as interpreted in the United States. His later mother, however, had a bad stroke in 1939 and died 22 years later in

1961. She was basically unable during this time to communicate with others. She could not walk unassisted. Her thinking was illogical and incoherent in general. Yet the concepts of nursing home, divorce, and separation never came up in the home setting. To the best possible her husband and three children took care of her and of the farming operations. Thus, the writer's mother would have no way of surviving by herself where the "survival of the fittest" and the "struggle for existence," as emphasised by Charles Darwin (1809-1882) would be in evidence. Rather, the philosophy of Thomas Henry Huxley (1825-1895) would have met more of her needs, as well as the needs today of the disadvantaged, the unemployed, the unemployable, and sickly in society. Huxley advocated improving the environment for all. This meant education, food, clothing, and shelter for all, should be adequate. Huxley's thinking is much more humane when dealing with human beings, as contrasted with Darwinian philosophy.

Huxley, of course, was not a communist or socialist. He merely looked to see what human beings needed to achieve, to attain, and to progress. The old question needs discussion in 1985 as to "Am I my brother's keeper?" This problem is stated in the book of Genesis when Cain rose up and slew his brother Abel. (Genesis 4: 3-11)

Heavy Defense Spending

Since 1981, the defense budget has soared in dollars. Generally, as each new presidential contender campaigned, rhetoric was used to emphasise how far ahead the other super power was in military capabilities. It is relatively easy to excite American people, and no doubt the Soviets, on "the enemy nation is coming to exercise world wide domination." Building fears such as that certainly can be carried to an excess. When individuals fear that when awakening tomorrow, seventeen Soviet soldiers will be there to enforce the latters will, it becomes quite ridiculous. Are there that many Soviet soldiers so each American home will be guarded by seventeen of their number? However, the writer believes that numerous Americans truly believe this to be true. In the United States and with the present administration, defense spending seems to be the only major goal on the federal level. The "big spenders" in Congress according to conservatives are those who wish adequate funding for domestic items, such as welfare needs of people, a clean environment, safe roads and highways, as well as a quality environment for all. The President and selected members of Congress seemingly can emphasise continual increased military spending and yet are not counted as the big spenders.

The more money spent on defense evidently makes for a safer United States, according to conservative and the new right thinking. Little, if any criticism is emphasised in spending $600 for each airplane toilet seat or $300 for a screwdriver or $300 for a single hammer in the military. These are items that make headlines in leading daily newspapers in the United States. What about other extreme wastes in defense spending that do not make even minor headlines? Certainly, without discipline in the amount of money spent for any institution be it the military or other in society, flabbiness, inefficiency, and corruption sets in.

Little is done in the area of negotiating between and among super powers. Fundamentalist electronic ministers tend to emphasise extremely heavy defense spending with little emphasis, if any, placed on negotiations. It would be difficult to find any passage in the Bible to support this point of view. It does not exist in Biblical content. There are passages that emphasise the opposite point of view, as is true of the following, (Matthew 5: 43-44).

43. Ye have heard that it hath been said, Thou shalt love thy neighbour, and hate thine enemy:

44. But I say unto you. Love your enemies, bless them that curse you, do good to them that hate you, and pray for them which despitefully use you, and persecute you.

45. That ye may be the children of your Father which is in heaven: for he maketh his sun to rise on the evil and on the good, and sendeth rain on the just and on the unjust.

46. For if ye love them which love you, what reward have ye? Do not even the publicans the same?
47. And if ye salute your brethren only, what do ye more than others? Do not even the publicans.

The writer at this point wishes to merely state that literal content in the Bible does not support United States foreign policy or the policy of any nation on the planet Earth at the present time. Mahatma Gandhi's policy of nonviolence in India toward Great Britain in the 1940's would come closest to emphasising content in The Sermon on the Mount. Equally so, in relating to other races in the United States, Dr. Martin Luther King also advocated and lived in a completely nonviolent way.

Creationism Versus Evaluation

Fundamentalist ministers tend to make much emphasis upon creationism taught in the public schools. They believe strongly that God created the natural environment, animal life, and human beings as presently in evidence. Little or no change has occurred in plant, animal and human life since Genesis was written with the statement "In the beginning, God created the heavens and the earth." With further statements of what was created in each of the six days of creation, God rested on the Sabbath. A six day creation was then involved. Literalists may state these were six 24 hours days. A few years ago Concordia Theological Seminary in St. Louis, Missouri split into factions. The conservative wing wanted seminary professors to teach that each of the six days of creation (24 hours per day) was exactly true as stated in the book of Genesis. There were no leeways nor interpretations other than those given in Genesis, chapter one. The more liberal professors and the president than of Concordia Theological Seminary felt they could not teach precisely the content desired by the conservatives.

Literal versus figurative interpretation is an old problem in theology and religion. The John Thomas Scopes trial of 1924 emphasised that Scopes, a biology teacher, taught evolution. Scopes left the teaching profession the following year. The pressure then was extremely great on both sides of the creationism versus evolution debate. William Jennings Bryan, who ran for the presidency three times and renowned statements in the United States, defended the creationist point of view in the Scopes trial. Clarence Darrow, one of the outstanding attorneys in the United States defended John Thomas Scopes. Both prosecution and defense had topnotch attorneys for the oppositing sides in the historic scopes trial of 1924. John Thomas Scopes was ultimately absolved from having violated the laws, rules and regulations of the state and nation.

A Three R's Curriculum

Conservatives of the New Right wish to have a basics curriculum with specific emphasis upon the three r's (reading, writing, and arithmetic). They believe that there are essentials for all students to master within the framework of the three r's. Selected conservatives may extend the basics to include science, social studies, the fine arts, and physical education. Frills and fads, however, are to be omitted in the curriculum.

The New Right would advocate that parents can inspect the curriculum and insist upon eliminating undersireable objectives and learning activities. Undersirable goals and content, as emphasised by the New Right, might well include the following:

1. values clarification strategies
2. critical and creative thinking of United States foreign policy
3. psychological testing of students
4. the teaching of evaluation
5. sex education
6. drug abuse instruction
7. problem solving strategies in the curriculum
8. teacher's unions and the National Education Association.

The New Right would favour:

1. group oral prayer in the classroom

2. instruction in creationism from the book of geneisis
3. traditional patriotism in the classroom
4. a Biblical Commonwealth, based on their beliefs.

The New Right:

1. blames public schools for drug abuse, easily obtained drugs (marijuana, heroine, cocaine, and alcoholic beverages, among others) in society are not blamed for drug abuse among junior and senior high schools in particular;
2. believes that vandalism and crime in the public schools is not caused. Vandalism and crime simply exists in the school setting. However, it must truly be said that highly negative happenings occur in society. The public schools cannot be immaculate as an island unto themselves;
3. stresses that public schools deliberately are not teaching and basics. Thus, graduates of the public schools cannot read, write or compute. Environmental forces then do not count in educating students.

The New Right needs to realise that peers, the home situation, friends, and income levels can make or break a students future. Opportunities need to be provided for students to learn. The student also must wish to learn. The classroom teacher must stimulate and provide readiness for learning.

In Closing

The New Right's rallying cry is to follow teachings found in the Bible in developing the ideal society. However, little of what fundamentalists advocate is found in the Bible. In fact, even with wide latitude in interpreting the Bible figuratively, justification for the thinking of fundamentalists cannot be found. Fundamentalists need to be challenged to state in which ways their beliefs relate even indirectly to content stated in the Bible.

20

Improving the Public School

There certainly has been a rash of criticism of the public (government) schools. These criticism include:

(a) teachers have not taught the basics. It is truly difficult to say which academic areas include the basics. Thus, it has become a slogan to "teach the basics," and eliminate frills and fads. Whether the major curriculum areas were ever minimised in teaching would be difficult to prove.

(b) discipline problems, vandalism, and drug abuse is in evidence in the public schools. Certainly, violence, crime and sales of harmful drugs is a problem in society. Hardly could an immaculate environment then be prevalent in the school environment. Too many budget cutters have cut down on the number of teacher in a school, thus hurting the quality of supervision needed in American schools. Too few teachers in the public school emphasise an excessive number of students to teach in any classroom.

(c) student achievement is down in the public schools. It takes quality teaching materials and up-to-date textbooks in helping pupils learn. Withholding state money to schools by governors and legislators certainly does not harmonise with improving the curriculum for students. It takes money, much money, to provide a learning environment conducive to guiding students to achieve as much as possible. The slogan "lets get government off our backs and out of our pockets" is not conducive in helping students learn to read, write, and compute at an effective level of achievement. Again, money is needed to educate students. Certainly, the Defense Department does not emphasise budget cutting to improve the military. Neither can public schools afford "that government" is best which governs least."

(d) schools are bureaucrats and dictate what is taught. Those writers in the news or in educational literature who include the term of bureaucracy (and related terms) as being negative generally lack understanding of content being written. Max Weber wrote very positively when advocating a bureaucracy as being an ideal in any business or educational establishment. A very small business or a small school system will have its hierarchy and thus a bureaucracy will be in evidence. Even in a democratic school system, decisions will be handed down from top to bottom, as well as group made decisions will be emphasised. There are federal, state, and district rulings which must be implemented in the school setting. Individual, as well as local decisions, cannot always be emphasised. Nor, is it desirable to do so. Certainly, anarchy would be an end result with each person doing as he/she wishes with no supervision or accountability.

Max Weber emphasised the following tenets in the bureaucracy:

1. Division of labour based on specialisation of talents.
2. Well-defined hierarchy of authority with superior-subordinate relations clearly and formally indicated.
3. A system of rules and regulations which clarify the rights and duties of all position incumbents.
4. A statement covering work to be performed.

5. Impersonality prevailing in interperson relations, that is, no favouritism to friends or those with special social status, and special emphasis on maintaining "social distance" between persons employed in positions at different levels in the organisational hierarchy.

5. A commitment to merit, objectivity determined in the selection and assignment of persons to various positions. Technical qualifications and past performances or experiences rather than political, social, family or other connections were to be used in position determination for persons employed.

Weber truly believed that a bureaucracy was the best way to organise a given group. Certainly, any organisation can become too anarchical where each does as they see fit. Also, any organisation (school or business) can become too hierarchical where decision making moves downward only from administrators to teachers.

(e) schools need to utilise common sense in teaching students. To a speaker or writer what has been said or written may be common sense to the beholder. It is surprising, however, on the many interpretations given as to what is the good life and what makes for a quality curriculum. Each of the following philosophical schools of thought, no doubt, emphasises a common sense approach:

1. the humanist who believes that students should be rather heavily involved in selecting objectives, learning activities, and evaluation procedures.

2. the behaviourist who emphasised predetermined measurably stated objectives selected by teachers prior to instruction.

3. the experimentalist who advocates students with teacher guidance selecting like-like problems to solve. Committee work is then emphasised in problem solving situations.

4. the structuralist who believes that academicions in their academic area of speciality identify major generalisations for teachers to emphasise in guiding students to achieve these structural ideas inductively.

It is quite obvious that a common sense approach does not exist in the school curriculum or in life.

Curriculum Improvement

What might then be done to improve the public school curriculum?

1. The lay public and parents, in particular need to support quality education. Supporting the public schools means to value learning in and of itself. A continuous barrage of criticism toward the public schools does not improve the curriculum. Rather, prizing opportunities to learn, progress, and achieve school be in evidence.

   To support quality education emphasises words, as well as deeds. Comments orally and in writing which speak positively of learning should assist students to increasingly master the basics, as well as other relevant curriculum areas. Negative statements about schools and learning can only hinder student progress.

   To encourage education in terms of deeds means that enough money must be available to reimburse teachers adequately in making a livelihood. Audio-visual aids, printed materials, and up-to-date textbooks need to be available to each pupil. It costs much money to have quality public schools. Budget cutting for education is costly. An increased number of illiterate, unemployed persons should not become a goal in the United States.

2. There needs to be more teacher input in terms of what should be done to improve the curriculum. The many studies that have been made in the United

States on how to improve education does not emphasise input from classroom teachers. The National Commission for Excellence in Education with their findings coming out in 1983 emphasised, among other things, the following:

(a) high school students should complete four years of English and three years each of science, mathematics, and the social studies.

(b) a longer school day, as well as a longer school year than is presently in evidence in American schools.

There are many weaknesses in recommendations such as the above listed items. There are secondary students that presently face problems in learning with three years of English, as well as one year each in science, mathematics and the social studies. Will adding additional years of required courses help learners who already have problems with a curriculum emphasising the academic areas? Very little was said in the National Commission for Excellence in Education report on vocational education for numerous high school students. Certainly, vocational education is a tradition in the United States and can be emphasised for the non-academically inclined student. It would be ridiculous to do away with vocational education, or greatly minimise it, in order to emphasise academic learnings heavily for all secondary students. The dropout rate of secondary students could indeed be great with a required academic curriculum for all students.

In Conclusion

There are numerous improvements that need to be made in American education. Economic and moral support for schools must be forthcoming from the societal arena. The following clipping from an Ann Landers column may well reveal what society prizes and wants from schooling and education:

Dear Ann Landers: My daughter is a high school sophomore. This fall she brought the 1984 yearbook.

I saw several photos of football players, cheerleaders, basketball games and various other sports. I also noted many pictures of the crowd at these events.

I could find to mention of the National Merit Scholarship finalists (the school have five), no picture of the girl who took her science fair project to the nationals, no picture of the award-winning problem-solving bowl team, no mention of the young man who presented a top-notch paper at the National Science Symposium. These major accomplishments went uncheered and unnoticed.

It is difficult to keep students interested in activities that require brain work if they get no recognition. Athletes, however, are virtually worshipped—not only at this school, but everywhere.

I hope the faculty advisors who supervise the yearbook for 1985 will give some space to students who have achieved something in the intellectual areas—Illinois.

Dear ill: Unfortunately, football and basketball are more exciting to most folks than a science fair project. They also bring in more money. I hope the faculty gives serious thought to what you have written. Your complaints have merit.

Professional teachers, under the circumstances, must do the best job possible in selecting quality objective, learning activities, and evaluation procedures for students.

21

Issues in Curriculum Development

There are numerous issues in developing the curriculum which have not been clarified in terms of meaning. Each issue needs to be clear and distinct from others. Selected issues will be described briefly with questions following.

The Charter School

Numerous writers in education as well as speakers proclaim the goodness of charter schools. Selected schools have implemented the charter school concept. Generally, charter schools are located within a public school system. A few may be located in empty school buildings or other suitable places. Charter schools tend not to be required to abide by state department standards like other public schools do. Administrators and teachers have received special permission from the state to be creative in curriculum, instruction, and evaluation.

To show higher pupil achievement in charter schools has been a problem. Which approaches to evaluate achievement should be used? The following procedures would indicate differences in pupil progress if one procedures is used as compared to another: standardised norm referenced tests, criterion referenced tests (CRTs), teacher written tests, checklists, and/or rating scales. A newer procedure is the portfolio and constructivism as a philosophy of evaluation.

Teachers, administrators differ much from each other in terms of which evaluation technique to use in appraising pupil achievement.

Questions that are arise pertaining to charter schools include the following:

1. If selected rules and regulations are to be waived for charter schools, why not for public schools in general? Detrimental rules should be taken off the books.
2. If smaller class size is to be in evidence for charter schools, why not have lower numbers per class for public school pupils?
3. If there is to be a dichotomy between charter versus public schools, why not provide the same benefits for each such as quality of building, materials of instruction, as well as funding?

Collaborative Learning

Collaborative learning is receiving much attention to enhance pupil achievement. Collaborative learning sounds much like committee work, a term that was popularised by John Dewey (1859-1952) in the early part of the twentieth century. Dewey believed that pupils liked working with others, as compared to working by the self in school work. His laboratory school at the University of Chicago in 1896 stressed cooperation rather than competition in involved learning activities. Dewey's flexible steps of problem solving are known by many educators.

Collaborative learning may be compared to individual tasks. Here, pupils choose or may be assigned work in ongoing lessons and units of study. Howard gardner in his Theory of Multiple Intelligences stresses nine areas of intelligence. Two of these that concern us here are interpersonal intelligence whereby pupils do well in committee or small group endeavours. In comparison to interpersonal intelligence is intrapersonal intelligence. Intrapersonal intelligence individuals may best show their intelligence by working individually on a project or activity. Thus, interpersonal versus intrapersonal school tasks becomes an issue. Perhaps, both can and should be emphasised in the school curriculum.

Questions that might be raised about pupils rather continuously working collaboratively are the following:

1. Is this the best way to help pupils achieved even though selected individuals prefer to work on lessons by themselves?
2. Should there be a rational balance between committee and individual tasks in the school curriculum?
3. Has collaborative work and its emphasis become a slogan in education?

Establishing Standards for Pupils to Achieve

Many states are now involved in setting standards for pupils to achieve. Educators on the state level are rather far removed from the local school setting. These standards become objectives for pupils on the local level to achieve. Learning activities for pupils are selected by the local teachers to guide learners to achieve objectives. Evaluation of pupil achievement is measured against the objectives by state developed tests to notice success in teaching and learning.

Frequently, the business world, among others, complains that pupils in public school do not achieve demanding objectives, as well as teachers not having high expectations for learners. Questions that may be raised pertaining to high standards in education set by the state include the following:

1. Should an external group, not involved in the local classroom, set standards for others to achieve? These people do not know the children being taught.
2. Are these externally developed standards more rigorous than those developed by the classroom teacher teaching involved pupils?
3. Who should make major decisions about what pupils are to learn.
4. Should the state level also determine learning activities to harmonise with the stated objectives? It does become difficult for the teacher in the classroom to find learning activities which harmonise with externally determined objectives.

5. How demanding should objectives be for pupils to objectives?

Testing Verses Portfolio Evaluation

Realism, as a philosophy of education desires precise test results from pupils in terms of per cent of items correct, percentiles, standard deviations, and stanine scores. An exact numeral is then to provide knowledge of how well a pupil is achieving.

Toward the other end of the spectrum are those emphasising more flexible procedures in appraising learner progress such as the portfolio. Inside the portfolio may be the following pupil products and processes:

1. written work of pupils covering content across the curriculum;
2. video and cassette tapes of oral communication of pupils;
3. samples of art work from diverse academic areas;
4. snapshots of projects and activities of pupils;
5. test results indicating learner progress.

Questions that may be raised pertaining to results of pupil achievement include the following:

1. How objective should pupil results of achievement be, such as numerals involving percentiles and standard deviations?
2. How objective can any evaluation technique be, such as in the case of standardised norm referenced tests? Human beings write the test item and choose what is to appear on the testing device.
3. Will portfolio results be subjective and lack internal reliability since different evaluators pass judgements on the contents therein?

The Interdisciplinary Curriculum

There is much written and said about the values of an interdisciplinary curriculum. There are selected curriculum areas that might correlate well such as history and literature. With cooperative planning and implementation, the history and literature teachers might come up with the following, as an example pertaining to a unit on the Civil War:

1. studying literature written during the Civil War;
2. examining primary sources written by individuals during the Civil War;
3. viewing contents of lyrics on songs of Civil War days.

An integrated curriculum might also be planned and implemented whereby one academic discipline provides the core of instruction. The following might serve as an example with history as the core academic discipline in a unit entitled "The Great Depression."

1. emphasising music written during the Great Depression;
2. Incorporating art products of the Great Depression;
3. stressing writings of the Great Depression;
4. bringing in discoveries in science;
5. fusing learnings and theories discovered by mathematicians.

Questions that might be raised pertaining to the interdisciplinary curriculum include the following:

1. to what extent should any academic or curriculum area be integrated?
2. might an academic discipline lose its identity with too much integration of subject matter?
3. can depth teaching be emphasised in one academic discipline when integration of subject matter is in evidence?
4. will there be inappropriate sequence for any academic discipline in an integrated curriculum?
5. might an academic discipline receive short schrift in integration and correlation?

How Should Objectives Be Stated?

There is considerable debate pertaining to stating objectives behaviourally as compared to more open ended procedures. Behaviourally stated objectives stress specificity in their writing. Thus, a pupil either does or does not achieve the objective as a result of teaching. After instruction, the teacher may appraise if a pupil has/has not been successful in achieving state objectives.

The objectives are written prior to instruction and may be announced to pupils before a lesson or instruction begins. Pupils then are more certain as to what is expected in terms of learning.

Toward the other end of the continuum, objectives for instruction might be much more open in order that diverse outcomes in pupil learning might be an end result. For example, with learning centres in the classroom, the pupil may select which centre to work at and which task to pursue. There should be more tasks at the diverse learning centres than what any pupil may pursue and complete. Why? Pupils individually might then omit tasks that do not possess perceived purpose. The learner is the chooser of which learning opportunities to complete.

Questions raised pertaining to behaviourally stated objectives might be the following:

1. can these objectives stress higher levels of cognition such as critical and creative thinking, as well as problem solving;
2. should pupils have more input into the curriculum such as in learner/teacher planning cooperatively of objectives, learner opportunities, and appraisal procedures?
3. does teaching becomes too hierarchical with preplanned objectives for pupils to achieve?

Questions that might be asked of open-ended, general objectives are the following:

1. does teaching become rather aimless with much leeway in objectives interpretation as to what will be taught?
2. how valid and reliable in evaluation when the objectives of instruction leave too much leeway for their learning(s)?
3. can learning opportunities be matched effectively with broadly stated objectives?

Conclusions

There are numerous issues in education which need identification. These issues need analysing to determine weaknesses with the intent of remedying deficiencies.

Pupil need to experience the best objectives, learning opportunities and evaluation techniques. Pupils possess, individually, diverse interests, purposes, and levels of achievement. It behooves the teacher to know and understand each pupil well so that teaching and learning might harmonise with each learner's styles and strengths. Pupils individually need to achieve as much as possible in achieving objectives.

22

Service Learning in the Community

Pupils need to develop a caring, belonging philosophy of education early in their school years. Objectives need to be framed carefully with adequate consideration. The worth of each end needs to be appraised thoroughly, prior to its implementation. Learning opportunities involving service in the community need to harmonise with the stated objectives. Thus, these learning opportunities need to be purposeful and on the achievement level of each learner.

Adequate evaluation needs to be emphasised in ascertaining if the objectives have been achieved. Techniques need to be valid and reliable, aligned with the stated objectives. Which learning opportunities might then be in the offing?

Learning Opportunities in Service Learning

There are diverse kinds of service learnings which may be adapted to the present achievement level of each pupil. One of my student teachers together with the cooperating teacher, whom I supervised, took her first grade pupils to a nearby nursing home where a programme was presented consisting of:

1. A song to the group.
2. A poem read by a pupil.
3. A story read cooperatively by two learners.
4. A dramatization on "The Three Billy Goats Gruff" presented by four pupils.
5. A story told of a picture drawn, related to an ongoing unit, an explained to nursing home residents.

The observers from the nursing home were very appreciative and enjoy having young people come.

A second student teacher and cooperating teacher I supervised believed that service learning started in the local classroom and on the school grounds. One rule in the classroom was to pick up all paper, dirt, and waste objects from the floor before going out to play or after school was out for the day. I must say the classroom was very clean. At the end of the school day all reference books were returned to their proper locations. Textbooks were put inside each pupils desks, as were scissors, crayons, paste, among other supplies, when the learning opportunity was completed or at the end of a class period whereby space was needed for the next sequential activity.

These same pupils with teacher guidance took turns keeping the playground free from paper, trash and debris. Thus, every fifth day, these second graders, kept the playground neat and tidy. For other classrooms took their turn in keeping the playground clean or sequential school days. Much pupil pride was shown over keeping the classroom and school grounds tidy.

Upper Grades and Service Learning

Upper grade pupils can do much to develop and maintain a service learning attitude. Thus, a third grade class with student teacher/cooperating teacher guidance sent pupils to a nearby nursing home, mentioned above, to read aloud to those senior citizens. Some of these elderly people cannot see well to read. Others find it difficult to concentrate while reading. Patients in the nursing home like to see and visit with school age pupils. They take much interest in being read to orally. These senior citizens requested books on a certain genre or even by title.

Third grade, here, appear to be well motivated to read aloud clearly and with voice inflection. They shared the illustrations with listeners as the read aloud continued. Nursing home patients asked to have selected titles read aloud again. Pupils tend to feel intrinsic rewards in service learning.

A student teacher together with the cooperating teacher planned with and took their fourth grade class to clean up a yard of a single parent who had cancer. The yard was located three blocks from the school. The home yard of the cancer patient was left in an immaculate condition. Safety was practiced by pupils and the teachers as trash and debris were picked up and placed in the pickup truck box. The single parent was very grateful to teachers and pupils for taking care of the lawn in ridding it of waste materials. In saying goodbye, the pupils sang, "The More We Get Together," to the cancer patient. This brought tears to her eyes. Pupils realised the difficult situation faced by some people. They had feelings of sympathy and empathy.

An interesting act of service learning was performed by a fifth grade student teacher and her cooperating teacher. As an involved team, they recognised the group to appear before the city council of the local city of 2,500 inhabitants. The city hall building was located four blocks from the school building. The purpose of the class appearance was to indicate the need for draining stagnant water, adjacent to the school grounds. The depression with stagnant water produced its supply of mosquitoes in early September. The principal strongly backed the school's attempts in service learning.

In a few days, there was a bulldozer which levelled the depression area and drove over the filled area several times to make the ground very solid. Young people can very successful in reconstructing the community!

What can sixth graders do in service learning? Here, a sixth grade student teacher and cooperating teacher developed purpose within their pupils to arrange displays at the local public library during *Reading Across America Week*. The following were set up in the local public library:

1. Two large bulletin board displays with captions and book jackets of Dr. Seuss books.
2. A printout of typed materials, researched on the life and times of Dr. Seuss.
3. Centres containing Dr. Seuss books written during each decade, 1940-50, 1951-60, 1961-70, 1971-80 and

1990 to the last book written. Each centre was neatly labelled together with interesting information on selected books.

4. Pupils as resource persons served at selected hours each day of *Read Across America Week.*

Selected pupils read books aloud to pre-school and primary grade pupils at the public library during *Read Across America Week*. These sixth graders also read to primary grade pupils in their respective classrooms during this same week.

Middle School Pupils and Service Learning

Middle school pupils are in the age range whereby many possibilities exist for service learning. I will list these pertaining to what my student teachers and their cooperating teachers emphasised in cities ranging from two thousand to eighteen thousand. The service learnings included the following:

1. Assisting food deliveries in Meals on Wheels programmes.
2. Working in a safe environment with Habitat for Humanity.
3. Helping at a clothing centre in which the clothes were available for the less fortunate.
4. Assorting donated food items at the local food pantry.
5. Shoveling snow to clear sidewalks for poor, elderly people.

In Closing

There are numerous opportunities for pupils in safe environment to engage in service learning. These learning opportunities should assist pupils to achieve carefully chosen objectives. Learners should realise that their very own personal needs should be met, and at the same time they are members in society. Needs and wants exist in the societal arena with its needy and unfortunate inhabitants. With feelings of respect, empathy, and caring, pupils need to realise that they should be of service to others. Hardships and difficulties among people in society need to be identified and possible solutions found.

23

Grouping Pupils for Instruction

There are numerous means of grouping pupils for instruction. Each approach needs to be appraised in terms of providing for pupils individually to realise optimal achievement. Teachers, principals and supervisors need to study, appraise, and implement that which assists each pupil to achieve optimally.

Groups have common properties. All groups have a *background* or lack of background which influences their behaviour. If children have worked together before, that joint work becomes part of their background. If not, this lack of prior contact will influence their interaction. People, including children, always approach group involvement with some kind of expectation. They may look forward to the experience, believing other people will contribute greatly to their investigation, or they may be unsure of how the group will work because they have little or no data on the members of the group.

In addition to background, all groups develop a *participation pattern* that exists over time and can be described at any particular moment. In a group of three children, for example, a pattern might emerge in which one child dominates the discussion with the other children listening attentively; in another group of three, there may be an equal exchange of views by each child.

All groups have the property of *communication*, which refers to how well members understand each other and how well they express their feelings, attitudes, and information. Children with very different cultural and/or experimental backgrounds may have difficulty making themselves understood by others in the group.

All groups exhibit *cohesion*, the bonds uniting the individual parts. Team spirit and group morale are outward signs of group cohesion.

Groups have the tendency to create *standards*, or rules of conduct necessary for remaining in the group. In social studies classes, the teacher may establish the standards and responsibilities for the group members. For example, he may appoint a group leader to keep noted that can be shared with the rest of the class. It is essential that everyone who participates in a group understood its standards, the expectations others have for each person's performance.

People in groups of three or more are often assigned particular roles that define the relationships among members. In these cases, the group has a particular *structure and organisation*. Sometimes the teacher assures a formal structure by assigning roles, and at other times allows the structure to remain informal, with roles and tasks shifting during different lessons. Sometimes the children's backgrounds and varying abilities determine group structure.

The Self-contained Classroom

In the self-contained classroom, one teacher generally teaches all curriculum areas (except perhaps, music, art, and physical education) to a single set of learners. Thus, the teacher selects objectives, learning activities, and evaluation procedures in the curriculum areas of language arts, social studies, science, mathematics and health.

Critics of the self-contained classroom concept believe that subject matter becomes too complex to have one teacher teach the majority of curriculum areas to a single set of pupils. This might be true on the intermediate grade levels, in particular. It follows that no teacher may have the competency or skill to teach so many diverse curriculum areas. Teachers then cannot acquire the needed skills to specialises in teaching a specific area of the curriculum in the self-contained classroom.

Advocates of the self-contained classroom believe that a teacher can do a good job of emphasising correlated, fused, and integrated means of curriculum organisation. These opportunities exist due to the self-contained teacher teaching most of the diverse curriculum areas to the single set of pupils. If the self-contained teacher wishes to, the separate subjects curriculum may also be emphasised. The self-contained classroom may emphasise a flexible means of scheduling for different curriculum areas. The teacher can divide the school day in terms of time needed specifically for each subject matter area. The self-contained teacher may also divide the school day into an even amount of time devoted to each curriculum area, as is true of departmentalised teaching. Flexibility certainly is possible when thinking of time given to each curriculum area in the self-contained classroom.

The teacher in a self-contained classroom has ample opportunities to get to know each pupil well. This knowledge should be utilised to increasingly do a better job of teacher, and thus more adequately provide for each individual learner.

There are selected facets of the self-contained classroom which need criteria to guide their effective implementation. The teacher needs to evaluate if he/she is keeping abreast of recommended procedures in teaching the language arts, social studies, mathematics, science, and health units. Pupils need to achieve optimally in each of these curriculum areas.

Departmentalisation and the Teacher

There are elementary schools which departmentalise diverse curriculum areas starting with the first grade level. Generally, departmentalisation is emphasised more so on the intermediate grade levels. In departmentalisation, the teacher may specialise in the teaching of a specific curriculum area. Thus, the teacher can became highly proficient in teaching language arts, science, mathematics, or social studies. Junior and senior high school teachers over the many years, in general, have taught in departmentalised schools.

Criticism that have been hurled against departmentalisation include the following:

1. pupils may perceive diverse curriculum areas as being fragmented and isolated rather than related to each other;
2. teachers may emphasise the teaching of subject matter to the minimising of attempting to get to know each pupil well;
3. teachers may not plan with other instructors to correlates, fuse, or integrate subject matter;
4. diverse periods in the school day may compartmentalise to an excessive degree that which is taught.

There are selected guidelines which need to be followed when implementing a quality departmentalised plan of instruction:

1. each teacher needs to study and implement recommended trends in his/her area of speciality in teaching pupils;
2. each teacher needs to plan with other instructors when it is feasible and good to correlate, fuse, and integrate diverse curriculum areas;
3. each teacher must attempt to get to know pupils well in order to assist each learner to achieve optimally.
4. depth, teaching of content in a specific curriculum area is recommended; however, learners should also develop generalisations pertaining to relating diverse curriculum areas.

Team Teaching and the Teacher

More minds are better than one mind in selecting objectives, learning activities, and appraisal techniques for a given set of pupils, according to the thinking of advocates of them teaching. A team must have at least two teachers as members. The emphasis here must be upon teachers in a team planning together the objectives, learning activities and evaluation procedures for teaching-learning situations. Teachers on a team might possess quite different philosophies of education. However, cooperation is a key concept to emphasise in teaming. Thus, one member must not dictate ends, means, and appraisal procedures to other members. In this is done, team endeavours are not in evidence. The ideas of each team member must be respected in planning an implementation sessions. There, perhaps, is no quicker way to defeat teaming approach than if respect for others is not in evidence. It may be necessary to place emphasis upon basis general agreements on philosophy of teaching approaches, as well as in acceptance of involved personalities when implementing team teaching approaches. A certain amount of harmony is needed between/ among team members if success in learning for pupils is to be a relevant end result.

Team members can learn from each other in planning sessions pertaining to teaching-learning strategies. Inservice education may then become an inherent part of team teaching. Each idea presented needs to be analysed in order to ultimately provide the best in experiences for pupils.

There may be a teaching team in which all members specialise in teaching a specific curriculum area, such as the language arts. An interdisciplinary team may also be involved in teaching a given set of pupils. Thus, a language arts teacher, a science teacher, and a social studies teacher may be members of one team.

Large group instruction, committee work, and individual study provide component parts in team teaching situations. Committee endeavours and individual projects and activities assist in clarifying that which was presented in large group sequential sessions.

Critics of team teaching state the following:

1. There are selected teachers who do a better job of teaching on an individual rather than a team basis.
2. Large group instruction methods do not provide adequately for individual differences.
3. It may be difficult for the team members to agree upon a given set of objectives, learning, activities, and appraisal procedures.

4. Pupils may not adjust well to several teachers as compared to an individual teacher in a self-contained room.

There, of course, are selected advantages given for advocating team approaches in teaching:

1. Members of a teaching team can learn from each other in sessions devoted to planning for teaching.
2. More than one teacher is involved in determining ends, means, and appraisal procedures in the curriculum. An improved curriculum might then result.
3. More than a single teacher is involved in planning learning activities, resulting in a variety of experiences for learners.
4. An integrated curriculum might truly be in the offering when team members represent diverse academic disciplines.

Interage Grouping

There are selected educators who emphasise pupils from several age levels working in a large group and committee endeavours. In society, younger, individuals, interact with older things. The school curriculum needs to emphasise that which harmonises with societal trends.

The Joplin (Missouri) plan of reading instruction emphasised interage grouping. Fourth, firth and sixth grade pupils were regrouped to form homogeneous units. Thus, a top group of achievers in reading might consist of selected fourth, fifth and sixth graders being taught in a specific classroom. Pupils chosen for any level of achievement in reading needed to be as homogeneous as possible within a classroom.

One might also perceive a set of first and second grade pupils working together at diverse learning centres. Each pupil then ideally selects sequential tasks to pursue. A learner may then select easier or more complex tasks to pursue depending upon interests, purposes, and abilities possessed. Individual as well as committee endeavours may be selected as tasks at diverse learning centres. Thus, interage grouping may well be in evidence when learning centres are utilised.

Disadvantages given for utilising interage grouping include the following:

1. State laws are in evidence as to when pupils enter the first grade level. Once this custom has started, it becomes increasingly complex to change to other forms of grouping pupils for instruction.
2. Older pupils may have learned to frown upon working with younger children. Attitudes developed by pupils may be difficult to change.

Advantage which might be listed for interage grouping include the following:

1. It seemingly is more lifelike for individual to interact with others of diverse age levels. Societal settings tend to encourage interage interactions.
2. Grade levels may mean very little when explaining achievement of individual pupils. Thus, a third grader, for example, may be a more proficient reader as compared to a sixth grade pupil.

The Nongraded School

The nongraded school philosophy does away with grade level designations. Thus, for example, it is inappropriate to speak about a pupil a being in grade one, two or three. Rather, toward the end of the kindergarten level of instruction, each pupil is evaluated in terms of present reading achievement levels. Teachers with principal leadership attempt to place each pupil for the next school year in terms of being in the top group, middle group, or the slowest group of achievers in reading. If a school has five roomfuls of six year olds, it is easier to group pupils homogeneously in reading achievement as compared to having two roomfuls of these learners only. The latter situation might make it very difficult to have two roomfuls of fairly homogeneous or uniform achievers in reaching. With three, four, or five roomfuls of six years old, educators in charge of grouping procedures can develop rather uniform levels of reaching achievement within each classroom. Even within a classroom, further efforts can be made to emphasise homogeneous grouping by dividing learners into three reading groups, with each ultimate group being as uniform as possible in achievement.

Each group of somewhat uniform achievers with teacher guidance attempts to continually realise optimal development. Thus, a top group of readers will increasingly continue to achieve new attainable goals. Slow learners with teacher assistance will not achieve as rapidly, by any means, in reading as compared to rapid achievers. However, slower achievers in reading will also be guided to achieve as much as possible utilising the best methods of teaching possible. Each teacher of reading needs to keep accurate records as to continuous sequential levels of achievement for each pupil. This is necessary so that a learner achievers continually and is successful in learning. The sky is the limit in terms of each pupil's attaining and accomplishing. Pupils, of course, must not be pursued to attain the unachievable.

What happens to twelve year old pupils who have completed six years of schooling beyond the kindergarten level and are reading on the ninth or tenth grade levels? Most of these learners will be entering the junior high years or middle school depending upon the philosophy of the involved school, where involved teachers may emphasise pupils working up to grade level standards. Thus, a talented pupil may actually be reading on the ninth or tenth grade levels, but the teacher might be teaching seventh grade level in the first year of junior high school. There certainly is a problem of sequence here. Ideally, the junior high school English teacher should notice which level the entering student is reading on and provide for continual, sequential growth.

What happens to the learner who completes six years of schooling beyond the kindergarten level in a nongraded school and reads on the fourth grade level of accomplishment? Grade level designations may be somewhat arbitrary in this discussion; however, the reader needs to have certain criteria to utilise when evaluating educational ideas.

The pupil reading on the fourth grade level of accomplishment enters the seventh grade, the first year of junior high school, and may be required to read to grade seven level. There certainly is a gap in terms of where the learner is presently in achievement (fourth grade) as compared to the desired level of the seventh grade, as emphasised by the involved English teacher. A traditional English teacher might have all seventh grade pupils read seventh grade literature assignments and requirements. Again, it is desirable if the seventh grade junior high school literature teacher accepts the learner where he/she is presently in reading achievement and provides for continuous optimal progress. There are high interest/low vocabulary materials which may be utilised in teaching reading to individual pupils who are reading on an achievement level lower than what is deemed desirable for average achievers.

Ragan and Shepherd list the following common features of most nongraded levels:

1. Continuous progress, vertical and horizontal movement, of pupils is provided for throughout the school year.
2. Curriculum articulation is provided by means of the identification of skills, knowledge and applications to be developed within a content area or areas over a wide span of years without a specific length of time being assigned to any portion of this span.
3. The pupil is positioned in the sequence based on his ability in and achievement of these skills, knowledges, and appreciations without regard for the number of years in school.
4. Extensive reporting and record-keeping system are developed between teachers and between teacher and parents.
5. A successful experience is provided for each pupil at his position with no failure or retention.

The Dual Progress Plan

Too frequently, pupils experience a self-contained classroom throughout the elementary school years, followed by an abrupt transition to a completely departmentalised, junior high school. Advocates of the dual progress plan of grouping believe that learners on the primary grade levels need to experience a self-contained setting. On the intermediate grade levels, pupils may then experience a dual situation, a self-contained classroom for language arts and social studies. Science and mathematics are taught in a departmentalised situation.

A teacher teaching both language arts and social studies may correlate the subject matter of these two curriculum areas. Also, the teacher may become very familiar with traits of learners when teaching language arts and social studies for a longer period of time to a given set of pupils as compared to a departmentalised situation. Flexible scheduling may also be utilised. More or less time may then be given to a language arts or to social studies as the need arises.

Since science and mathematics are taught in a departmentalised setting, a teacher may specialise in teaching a specific curriculum area. Thus, a teacher having adequate background of class work in mathematics and an elementary education major may teach mathematics only, in the elementary school. The individual teacher may then specialise in teaching a specific curriculum areas. Or, a teacher with a double major, science and elementary education, may then utilise his/her strengths in teaching science only, to elementary school pupils.

Too frequently, in the elementary school, a teacher cannot specialise in teaching a specific curriculum area. The dual progress plan provides opportunities for departmentalised teaching. The dual progress plan of instruction also offers opportunities to teach in a modified form of the self-contained classroom. A teacher may then teach language arts and social studies to a given set of learners.

Heterogeneous Versus Homogeneous Grouping

A long debate has been in evidence for some time pertaining to which plan of grouping pupils for instruction is better—heterogeneous of homogeneous grouping. In heterogenous grouping of learners for instructional purposes, mixed capacity and achievement levels are present in a single classroom. Slow, average, and fast learners within a classroom might then experience learning activities cooperatively. Within each classroom, heterogeneously grouped pupils may also be separated into specific achievement level groupings for instruction in reading and other curriculum areas, as this is desirable. However, ample opportunities exist in a heterogeneously grouped classroom for learners of diverse achievement levels to interact and learn from each other in an atmosphere of respect.

Advantages given for emphasising heterogeneous grouping of learning for instruction include the following:

1. Democracy is in evidence when pupils who possess diverse differences are not segregated from each other, but have ample chances to learn from each other, as well as develop positive attitudes to others.
2. Society emphasises that individuals interact with each other regardless of capacity and achievement levels. Thus, the school setting must implement strategies in which individuals learn to live together harmoniously with others regardless of capability traits possessed.

Homogeneous grouping emphasises that pupils similar in achievement be taught together in a single class setting. An entire classroom of pupils may be talented and gifted. Or, an entire classroom of learners may be homogeneous as to being slow learners in reading. Too frequently, it is felt that gifted/talented learners are held back in achievement by those not learning content as rapidly. Toward the other end of the continuum, slow learners may feel frustrated when comparing themselves with high achievers in a heterogeneously grouped classroom. A homogeneously grouped class is somewhat uniform in terms of pupil progress. Thus, in homogeneous grouping a slow learner may not compare himself/herself with others who progress at a more rapid rate in a specific class setting. Or, a fast learner does not need to be held back in accomplishing due to a teacher gearing instruction toward average achievers or slow learners.

Numerous teachers prefer to teach in homogeneously grouped classroom. The range of pupil achievement is less in a homogeneously grouped class as compared to a heterogeneously grouped set of learners. It might be easier then to provide for optimal achievement on the part of pupils in a homogeneously grouped teaching-learning situation.

Knezevich wrote:

After admission and enrolment, pupils must be classified for instructional purposes. Perhaps the most significant change in the classification of pupils came with the grading of the elementary schools in Boston in 1847. Such grading today represents merely a rough attempt at grouping pupils for the purposes of instruction. Further classification is necessary when there are more than enough pupils to fill one grade room or one high school class section, and considerable attention has been devoted to developing methods of grouping that will facilities the learning or the teaching process.

Heterogeneous grouping can be defined as class sectioning on the basis of chance factors or arbitrary standards unrelated to learning ability or past performance. Homogeneous grouping implies placement of pupils into class section on the basis of some measure of ability. Because it is impossible to organise a section or grade in which all students have the same kind and quantity of ability or social background, "homogeneous" implies *approximately* the same kind and quality of ability as measured by some instrument. Stated another way, the range of some type of student ability is less in a homogeneous than in a heterogeneous section.

With increased mainstreaming of selected special education pupils into the regular classroom, less emphasis might be in evidence presently for advocating homogeneous grouping of pupils. Mainstreaming emphasises placing special education pupils in the least restricted environment. No longer may all special education pupils be segregated from other pupils in the regular classroom. Thus, a blind or partially sighted pupil may receive instruction in the regular classroom setting. Individual Education Programmes (IEP's) need to be written for each mainstreamed student. Parents ideally need to approve the IEP's for their child before their implementation. The IEP's consist of sequential measurably stated objectives for each pupil to achieve. Observable evidence is necessary to determine if the specific ends have been attained. There are pros and cons in administering mainstreamed programmes of instruction.

Advantages given include the following:

1. Special education pupils are not as a separated from other learners as was true previously.
2. A democratic society does not emphasise hierarchical arrangements of individuals.

Disadvantages which might be listed for mainstreaming of pupils may include the following:

1. Teachers in a regular classroom are not educated/ trained to teach special education pupils.
2. Much paper work is involved in writing IEP's and providing evidence of learner achievement.
3. It is difficult for the teacher to provide for individual differences when the range of pupil achievement in a classroom is great.

Salzer and Drdek wrote the following:

The placement of handicapped children in normal classes may be viewed as helpful to all concerned—the pupils with difficulties have the opportunity to learn how to function in a realistic situation, and the other children are helped to realise that classmates with special problems are more like them than they are different. For some of the reasons it may be argued that the extremely bright and able pupil is also better off in a class of normal children, especially if the classroom programme is flexibly organised so that individualised work is possible.

When children who are socially handicapped in areas of vision, hearing, speech, mental ability, or mobility are placed in regular classrooms, the demands made on the teacher undoubtedly increase. But with the help of resource people who know how to meet the difficulties that arise, the situation can be handled in ways which benefit all the pupils. Another desirable outcome is that the teacher, in working to meet the special needs of one or two pupils, may become more sensitive to the individually of all children.

Learning Centres and Open Space Education

A flexible means of grouping learners involve the utilisation of learning centres. Learning centres may be set up in a single classroom using the services of a single teacher. Learning centres may also be in evidence among diverse sets of pupils taught be a team of teachers in an open space area. Philosophical ideas to support the use of learning centres, among others, include the following:

1. Learners make decisions in terms of what to learn sequentially rather than emphasising a teacher-determined curriculum.
2. Trust between and among teachers and pupils is necessary if the latter are to truly make choices and decisions.
3. A humane learning environment exists when pupils are involved in deciding the ends and means of learning.
4. Pupils need to accept consequences of choices made.
5. Each learner needs opportunities to fulfil personal interests rather than sole purpose of the teacher.
6. Pupils need to make decisions presently rather than waiting for a future optimal adult time to enter the choice making arena.

There are numerous learning centres which the teacher might develop on his or her own. Within the flexible framework of these centres, pupils may select what to learn sequentially. Or, teacher-pupil planning might be heavily implemented to decide upon the objectives and learning activities of each centre. No doubt, teacher/pupil planning is significant in choosing tasks for each centre. Time factors may make it difficult to advocate involved teacher-pupil planning for each learning centre. Even if the teacher determines ends and means for each learning centre, the pupil must still have an open-minded curriculum to accept or reject sequential tasks to complete. The pupil ideally must always be a busy learner. There are enough tasks for each learner to continually work on, and yet perceived purposeless tasks can be omitted.

The following are examples of tasks for pupils to select and complete at one learning centre:

1. Read a library book of your choosing. Draw a picture pertaining to what was read.
2. Make a relief map showing the setting of the completed library book.
3. View a filmstrip and write five main ideas of what was viewed.
4. Select a picture from the file and write a related poem.
5. Construct a model colonial village.

An unit of study can be subdivided into various titles for learning centres. Among others, the following, for example, could provide titles for learning centres:

1. a reading centre
2. dramatization centre
3. poetry writing centre
4. speaking centre
5. art centre
6. music centre
7. creative story writing centre
8. construction centre
9. processing centre
10. interviewing centre

Each learning centre should possess a creative title. Instead of having the following above named titles, a reading centre, dramatisation centre, and poetry writing centre, the teacher may creatively have as labels— "Let's Enjoy Reading," "We Dramatize our Experiences," and "Let's Write Poetry."

Each centre needs to have concrete, semi-concrete, and abstract learning activities to help each learner achieve at an optimal level. Activities encountered should stimulate pupils to develop interest, purpose, and meaning in ongoing units of study.

In Conclusion

There are diverse recommended procedures in grouping pupils for instruction. Each plans needs to be appraised in terms of assisting pupils individually to achieve optimally in intellectual, social, physical, and emotional development. Thus, each of the following plans, among others, in grouping learners for teaching-learning situations needs evaluating:

1. the self-contained classroom
2. departmentalisation
3. team teaching
4. interage grouping
5. the nongraded school
6. the dual progress plan
7. heterogeneous versus homogeneous grouping
8. learning centres and open space education.

Questions for Consideration

1. Visit an elementary school to notice how pupils are grouped for instruction. In your own thinking, which revisions, if any, for grouping learners would you make? Justify your reasons in terms of recommended criteria.
2. Discuss with the classroom teacher, as well as the school principal, which methods of grouping pupils they would recommend if personal choices could truly be made.

3. **Survey recent literature involving methods of grouping learners for instruction. Which conclusions did you realise in your survey?**

REFERENCES

1. Cunningham, LaVern. *"Team Teaching and Large Group Instruction,"* Magnetic Recording. St. Paul, Minnesota: Minnesota Mining and Manufacturing Company, No Date.

2. Doll, Ronand C, *Curriculum Improvement*. Boston: Allyn and Bacon, Inc., 1978.

3. Ediger, Marlow, *The Elementary Curriculum, A Handbook*. Kirksville, Missouri: Simpson Publishing Company, 1977.

4. Flanders, Ned A. *Analysing Teaching Behaviour*. Reading, Massachusetts: Addison-Wesley Publishing Company, 1970.

5. Hunkins, Francis P., Jan Jeter, and Phyllis Maxey. *Social Studies in Elementary Schools*. Columbus, Ohio: Charles E. Merrill Publishing Company, 1982.

6. Knezevich, Stephen J. *Administration of Public Education*. New York: Harper and Row, 1975.

7. Popham, James, *How to Prepare Teaching Performance Tests*. Filmstrip and Cassette. Vincet Associates, 1972.

8. Ragan, William B., and Gene Shepheard, *Modern Elementary Curriculum*. Fifth Edition. New York: Holt, Rinehart and Winston, 1977.

9. Roe, William H., and Thelbert L. Drake. *The Principalship*. Second Edition. New York: Macmillan Publishing Company, 1980.

10. Salzer, Richard T., and Richard E. Drdek, "Organising for Learning" Chapter Three in *Curriculum for the Modern Elementary School*, Walter T. Petty (Editor). Chicago: Rand McNally College Publishing Company, 1976.

11. Wiles, Kimball, and John T. Lovell. *Supervision for Better Schools*. Fourth Edition. Englewood Cliffs: Prentice-Hall, Inc., 1975.

24

Guidelines for Helping the Child Learn

There are guidelines to follow in assisting their child to learn. These guidelines, when followed will help the child to learn more effectively. They are not difficult to follow, but can be readily applied when assisting the child to learn in any subject matter area. It is important to have the child learn as much as possible for many reasons, including the following:

1. the world is becoming a more complex place to live in. New inventions and ideas keep coming in and need to be accepted, if they are positive. The use of the computer is one example of an invention which has come in and taken over much of the work formerly done by hand such as in computing and writing by hand. Each pupil needs to stay updated and not be left behind.
2. the level of formal education attained by each person is increasing. With a more complex world, it is necessary to obtain as much formal education as possible. Informal education, outside the classroom, is also important. Much can be learned from reading print materials on one's own, visiting museums, and observations made in the out of doors.
3. more training is necessary on the job in terms of inservice programmes is necessary. Inservice education is there to help the individual develop and maintain knowledge and skills.

4. change is an important concept to consider and keep in mind. What is emphasised presently may be subject to change. Change may come about very quickly. Not everything changes at the same rate. Generally, what is new is better than what existed a few years ago. Automobiles, computers, and appliances, as examples, have improved much. Hardly do automobiles give problems whereby the car is stalled by the roadside. The author well remembers in the 1940s how cars with flat tires were parked by the side of the road with the owner patching tires. Fuel pumps gave out as did the points in the ignition system. This has all been improved upon with fuel injection and an electronically controlled ignition system. Very few stalled cars exist on the roadside. Methods of teaching have changed also. Most schools have been equipped with computer systems for use in instruction in the classroom as well as for other school tasks. Change must not be shunned but rather evaluated to have it go in the direction of benefiting human beings.

5. what is considered good at one time is no longer satisfactory. Expectations for what is a literate person has undergone many modifications. When attending high school in the 1940s, the author perceived an illiterate person to be one who could not read or write, period. Now, at James Madison High School, Arlington, Virginia, a student on the eleventh grade is to be able to read on the eleventh grade level. This is an expectation by the 2010 school year! If a pupil can read on the eleventh grade level, he/she can read almost everything which would be of personal interest and maturity.

   A person should also be literate in social studies and science. What happens in any area of the world affects people on the local level be it wars in Vietnam and Iraq or economic factors. The social studies has vital contributions then to make in developing the educated individual. Also, any person lives in a world of science. Science is with us continually such as in air which is breathed, soil used for food production and building purposes, trees used for a supply of lumber, petroleum valuable for automobile use, among others. Certainly with state mandated objectives for testing pupils in the public schools, reading and mathematics alone should not receive attention only, but social studies and science should be equally salient.

6. provision also needs to be made for those who are not academically, inclined. These individuals may be future skilled carpet layers carpenters, brick layers, computer technicians, automobile repair personnel, appliance repair persons, and plumbers, among other vital service individuals. The above name are extremely important in society. These people, too, need to be able to read well and be capable in mathematics.

7. general education is necessary for all. To be a good citizen means to be an informed person in order to play a vital role in society. There are salient responsibilities in being a responsible member in society. To live within the law is a necessity in order for society for function well. Then too, each person should be available to hold office, if asked to do so. Local positions may be quite satisfying to the individual including the following organisations:

   - being an officer in a local club, no matter what the size of the organisation is.
   - attending school board and city council meetings as children and as adults. A few aspire and do become a member of the school board or city council. One can become an active member in society in different ways including campaigning for a school board member during election time. There are individuals who give massive

amounts of time in campaigning for a candidate of their rational choice. Involvement, in some possible way is important.

- assisting with Boy Scouts, Girls Scouts, religious groups, and other youth organisations.
- helping to get school sponsored food baskets ready for the needy at holiday time.

8. physical fitness and good health are vital for all in society. Health insurance costs rise due to improper diets and a lack of exercise by numerous individuals. To do well in life, good health is needed. Much is demanded from able persons in society. They need to accomplish and achieve. There is much work to be done to make for a cleaner, healthier, safer environment. Good health should be a goal for all to achieve.

So much for stating how important it is for pupils to do well in school and receive the best education possible. Next, how pupils learn at home needs to be considered. First, parents need to read aloud to young children. This is one way for children to notice how interesting it can be to be a good reader. The enjoyment of hearing the content read and view the related illustrations truly can make for an enjoyable experience. Good attitudes toward literature is an important factor in having pupils learn to read and read well. As soon as the infant can sit on the parent's lap, reading aloud to young children should be in the offing. The young child should not be forced to listen. With proper use of the voice, the parent can lengthen the attention span of the child. Voice use involves reading with inflection, not with a monotone voice. Sharing with the child in a loving one to one relationship alone is satisfying. The parent's time belongs to the child alone. Psychologically, this is a very sound practice. As the child matures, the attention span will increase in length.

Second, the subject matter read to the child in the home setting needs to be engaging. The pupil must like to hear the subject matter read. Choosing books or rereading library books which children enjoy is very beneficial to the latter. It does not take long for a parent to notice which library book content is enjoyable for the child. The young child will push the less liked books to the side. Books liked by the child will increase attention span as well as increase knowledge possessed by the young learner. The school has one role, among others, which is vital and that is to assist each pupil to increase his/her fund of knowledge. The parent needs to watch the child to notice which kinds of literature are liked and which are not as interesting. The interesting kinds of subject matter should be read to young children.

Third, motivation for the pupil is salient. The parent needs to encourage the young child to listen to good literature being read. Kindness and acceptance of the child is relevant. Too frequently when the child is actually reading with the help of the parent, the latter may expect too much of the pupil. The expectations should be reasonable and encouraging, not frustrating. Scolding and reprimanding should be eliminated. The young child, rather, needs to feel that he/she can succeed and then does become a successful reader. The parent must help the child develop this feeing. Success in reading should be followed with the child actually experiencing increased feelings of being successful. The parent needs to observe the child to notice how difficult or easy the subject matter to be read should be. Judgement can be made on the subject matter to be read once the parent has observed the child and notices what the child likes and can understand as well as enjoy. Enjoyment will be a key factor for the child in learning to read as well as to keep on reading. The reading materials need to be child centred. Enjoyment can make for motivation to read children's literature.

Fourth, parents need to help each child feel that there is a purpose in learning to read. The young child will let the parent know which library books are to be read to him or her and which are not liked. When our grandchild was two years old, the father had six short library books ready for oral reading. The grandchild immediately tossed aside two least liked books. The father read aloud to the child the remaining four illustrated books. The child liked the read aloud and then picked up the two library books from the floor for oral reading also! Sometimes, the young child does not want to hear a library book read again. Each child has his/her preferences as do adults. If a child brings a library book to the parent for reading, the latter needs to take time out from his/her busy schedule to take advantage of this golden opportunity to fulfil a child's purpose in reading.

Fifth, understanding of content read is important. The child does not read words alone, but also attaches meaning to what has been read. It is salient to identify words correctly while reading, but it is also important to have the words stand for subject matter read. Being a word caller is not adequate in and of itself. Words make sense only if they relate to a larger whole and that is a sentence or paragraph. The words identified may help to make for a complete story.

The author has made introductory points about the importance of parents helping the child to become a good reader. Also, selected criteria were mentioned for parents to assist the child in actual reading, be it in beginning reading or beyond the introductory phases.

Which then are specific methods a parent may use to help a young child in word recognition? The child needs to be ready for the use of these techniques. How does a parent know if a child is ready?

1. the child asks many questions about how to pronounce words by pointing to them individually, in print. Being curious about words and their correct pronunciation is a clue to the parent that the child is becoming increasingly ready to identify new words. Then too, the chances are the child will indicate he/she has learned to pronounce words correctly from reading lessons in schools. There should be no forcing of a child in using these techniques. Why? Reading is pleasant experience, not one to be abhorred. When the child is ready, a parent should read a selection such as an interesting, easy, story, short in length. The parent points to the words as they are being read slowly and clearly. Next, the parent and child should

read the same selection together. Rereading can be done as often as the child is interested in doing so. Here, the child will usually learn to identify many words by sight.

2. the child is asking questions about a story read to him/her. Each question needs to be carefully considered and acknowledged. Wanting to discuss ideas from reading is marvelous. At all age levels what has been read needs to be discussed to clarify ideas. It is also enjoyable to talk about content read. If the young child begins to relate one story to another, this is excellent. He/she is then remembering content read as well as noticing that there are similarities and differences in stories read. Later on the learner will make more critical comparisons in subject matter read. This is a wholesome sign in that the child is retaining more of what is and has been read as well as recalling what to compare with connections being made.

3. the child wants to do some of the reading whereas formerly the parent did all of the oral reading. When the child can identify words correctly within the context of the parent reading aloud to the child, several factors are noted. The child can follow along in the printed script as the parent reads aloud. The child has a desire in learning to read. Wanting to learn to read is an important factor. There are high school graduates who never learned to read until they wanted to learn to do so and came to a facility offering free reading instruction to adult non-readers. Being older and more mature in wanting to learn to read, the adult is starting to develop needed basis skills. The wanting to learn to read is an important factor.

4. the child increasingly reads the content to the parent but needs some assistance in word pronunciation and identification. He/she indicates how far along he/she is in reading achievement. Generally, a child will want to continue to reveal progress in reading as readiness permits.

5. the child tells how two words begin alike or two words end alike. This number can increase to two or more as reading literacy increases.
6. he child is beginning to look carefully at vowel letters and how the same vowel letters may be alike or different in sound.
7. the child is able to hear long and short vowel sounds.
8. the child notices irregularities in sound/symbol relationships in consonant symbols.
9. the child may notice the schwa sound, be able to blend consonants, notice patterns in spelling and notice how the letter "r" governs the letter "e" in sound.
10. the child develops skill in retelling a story.
11. the child is able to develop a different beginning for a story. This experiences creative thinking. It is good to have children come up with unique and novel ideas in reading subject matter.
12. the child asks questions about the story. These questions might pertain to the character(s), the setting, the plot, the theme, among other literary devices.
13. the child assesses what he/she liked and/or disliked about the story read.
14. the child wishes to pantomime a part of the story.
15. the child desires to creatively dramatise the story just read.

The above enumerated items may not always follow in the ordered sequence. They do provide the parent with guidelines in terms of which selected reading skills to emphasise. The child will provide information as to which skill should be stressed sequentially, that is first, second, third and so on. The parent needs to study the child to learn which titles are of interest to read aloud together. The child will also give feedback to the parent in terms of how difficult the contents of a library book should be for the read aloud. Children are unique begins; no two are alike. That is what makes a study of people so interesting! There are children who learn to recognise words without phonics instruction. There are others who benefit from phonics providing that there is consistency between symbol and sound. When all is said and done, the child needs to learn the contents of the library book and enjoy the togetherness activity with the parent. Being together with the parent in a caring one on one relationship truly is very satisfying to the child, psychologically. This caring and close relationship alone should create for the child a desire to be read to and to enjoy reading library books.

25

Recommendations in Education, Are There Weaknesses Here?

In surveying literature on teaching and learning, there are selected concepts that come up very frequently. These same concepts appear from at teacher education conference. Which concepts are mentioned most frequently?

1. need for staff development
2. pupil collaboration and committee work
3. parental involvement in schools
4. higher standards for pupil attainment
5. heterogeneous grouping of pupils
6. hands on approaches in learning
7. problem solving and the curriculum
8. mentor teachers
9. mainstreaming of pupils (full inclusion)
10. portfolios and evaluation.

I will be briefly explain each of the above named concepts in terms of selected ideas in each. This will be followed by questions involving the issues surrounding what is recommended in literature pertaining to education, teaching, and learning.

Need for Staff Development

Writers in education write in a normative manner stressing what is and what should be in many facets of improving the public schools. These writing include the above ten enumerated concepts as well as multicultural education, a community of learners, school and university cooperation, field based teacher education, among many others.

For each concept stressed in educational writings, staff development is mentioned in the journal article. Thus, in emphasising any innovation, inservice education of teachers is necessary.

Questions that need answering pertaining to staff development and inservice education are the following:

1. What would have "to give" if there were teacher training in each area? There certainly would be much more time given to workshops, faculty meetings, and other forms of teachers education. Would this improve the public school or take preparation time for lesson and unit development away from teachers?
2. How much of new concepts written about in educational literature might teachers implement, if perceived worthwhile, on their very own violation? Each school should have a professional library for teachers to use on their very own in reading about innovation in the public schools.
3. Are teachers responsible individuals or does some outside source need to determine what is deficient in teaching.

Pupils Collaboration and Committee Work

An increased number of writers stress pupils working together continuously with others in a group setting in the classroom. Research is very often quoted to substantiate collaborative endeavours. Cooperative learning is a somewhat synonymous term with collaboration or committee endeavours. Actually, committee endeavours were advocated and implemented by John Dewey in his Laboratory School in 1896, connected with the University of Chicago.

The following needs discussion and debate pertaining to pupils engaged in cooperative learning:

1. What kind of rational balance should be placed upon cooperative learning (interpersonal) as compared to individual projects and activities (intrapersonal endeavours) by the teacher? Howard Gardner, Professor of Psychology at Harvard University, states that interpersonal as compared to intrapersonal talents comprise two of eight intelligences possessed by pupils.
2. Even if research states that pupils in Experimental Groups with cooperative learning do better at the .05 level of statistical significance as compared to Control Groups with traditional approaches in placing pupils into diverse grouping patterns, does that warrant all pupils working collaboratively? In any experimental group doing better than the control, there still are individuals using the innovative approach that do not do as well as those in Control Group. Gifted/talented pupils may do most or all of the work in committee endeavours.
3. Are teachers more skilled in teaching when traditional procedures are used in teaching and yet individual differences are being met? Here, phonics versus whole language approaches in teaching reading may be discussed. I believe in observing *what* pupils need. Some need more of phonics in identifying unknown words as compared to others.

Parental Involvement in Schools

Having parental involvement in schools has become an Absolute in writings on teaching and learning. To be sure, there is much that parents can do to assist pupil achievement. Thus reading to pupils, listening to pupils read, and talking about what was read can certainly help many pupils to do better in school. Parents may also help out in the classroom by pronouncing unknown words to pupils who are reading from library and textbooks. I have observed a parent doing an excellent job of assisting a small group of pupils in word recognition. Sometimes, grandparents have come to the classroom to help pupils, such as in a respectful manner supervising the development of a bulletin board in social affairs. A parent or grandparent may have had former teaching experience and can do much to assist teachers in many curriculum areas. One former teacher helped pupils with science experiments on air pressure. The examples certainly can be numerous on good ways that parents and grandparents have helped out in the classroom.

The opposite end of the continuum has also happened whereby parents have had very negative influence in the home and school. I will mention a few of these in school. One parent whose son had done much disrupting in the classroom kicked, rather viciously, the regular teacher and the lead teacher on the shins. These kicks had produced considerable pain, lasting through the following day. As the boy did the kicking, the mother said nothing. It appeared as if she approved of the kicking. A daughter who caused negative uproars in the classroom called the regular teacher and lead teacher "liars." The mother merely said in a sweet, soft voice, "Nina, we shouldn't do that." I felt the mother certainly approved of the girl's name calling of teachers. Many teachers have experienced these nightmare situations. There are parents who neglect their children, physically and sexually abuse their children, as well as engage in other hurtful situations.

I remember two graduate students in my class who were regular teachers making the following statements, one per student:

1. How do you did rid of a parent's help that is hurting the children in the classroom?
2. How do you control an aggressive parent who wishes to take over the classroom?

As educators, we need to ponder over questions pertaining to the role of parents in the school setting. Questions that arise are the following:

1. How can parents be selected who will truly be a positive influence to children?
2. What can be done with parental help that is not beneficial to the pupils and the teachers?
3. Which kinds of inservice education would guide parents to help pupils in school in a positive manner?

Higher Standards for Pupils to Achieve

There are numerous writings in education on setting high standards or objectives for pupils to attain. A major reason given here for setting high standards is to help pupils achieve at a higher level in all curriculum areas. It is felt that pupils are not doing well in school achievement.

Questions that may be raised pertaining to setting high standards for pupils to achieve, usually developed on the state level include the following:

1. How high school standards be set for pupils to achieve?
2. Are educators on the state level in a position to know what pupils can achieve on any grade level? They are far removed from the local classroom where these standards would be implemented.
3. Can suitable learning opportunities be located by teachers to guide pupils in achieving these objectives? This may present problems in a school where teaching materials are limited.

Heterogeneous Grouping of Pupils

Many educators recommend that only heterogeneous grouping of pupils be emphasised. Heterogenous grouping empasises mixed achievement levels of pupils in any classroom. Seemingly, educators who have their manuscripts in print frown strongly on homogenous grouping or "tracking" or pupils.

Questions that might be raised about heterogeneous grouping include the following:

1. How are gifted or talented pupils affected by heterogeneous grouping in the classroom?
2. Can a teacher assist *all* to do well in the classroom if the range of pupil achievement is great, such as in heterogeneous grouping?
3. Might there not be a combination of heterogeneous and homogeneous grouping in a classroom whereby each learner is helped to learn as much as possible?

Hands-on Learning

Many educators advocate a hands-on approach in learning. Learning by doing is then being emphasised. Concrete and semi-concrete materials of instruction then predominate. Experiments, demonstrations, construction activities, project methods, dramatic opportunities, and making items related to ongoing lessons and units of study would emphasise a hands-on approach in learning. There are numerous questions which may be identified here.

1. What kind of balance should there be between hands-on learning as compared to the use of semi-concrete and abstract materials of instruction?
2. Can reading across the curriculum be stressed, when heavy emphasis is placed upon hands-on approaches in learning?
3. Might hands-on learning be a perquisite or readness for reading on going lessons and units of study? There is more to learning, in addition to hands-on approaches.

Problem Solving in the Curriculum

How much emphasis should problem solving receive in teaching-learning situations? Dewey (1915) advocated problem solving in his Laboratory School at the University of Chicago in 1836. Here, pupils identified real problems faced in the societal arena. They developed an hypothesis as a temporary answer to the problem. Information was gathered to test the hypothesis in a life-like situation. The hypothesis was revised, if necessary. The problem solving approach advocated by Dewey was based on reality and reality based situations, not abstract experiences. These problems were not word or story problems from a basal textbook. Problems involved perplexity in terms of uncertainty in learning as to which path to pursue.

Questions involving problem solving are the following:

1. Since people in society are continuously identifying problems to solve, why don't teachers emphasise life-like problem solving in the classroom?
2. Are there too many pupils in a classroom to truly stress problem solving in the curriculum?
3. Do parents accept the importance of problem solving activities? There is a tendency to emphasise the basics, on the part of parents.

Mentor Teachers

Mentor teachers are experienced teachers with good track records in teaching. They are able to work together well in supervising beginning teachers. This provides beginning teachers with opportunities in grow, develop, and achieve. Many problems and difficulties may be avoided by the beginning teacher who is well supervised by a quality mentor.

Questions that arise pertaining to mentor teacher assistance of beginning teachers are the following:

1. Do mentors achieve well in relating effectively to beginning teachers?
2. What about the feelings of beginning teachers who would rather work alone with pupils in the classroom, without mentor assistance?
3. Might there be mentors who keep beginning teacher from doing well in the classroom?

Mainstreaming of Pupils

It is a common approach presently to have special education pupils placed into the regular classroom. Thus the mentally retarded, the autistic, and the behaviourally disordered may be taught with normal children in the classroom.

PL 94-142, a federal mandate of 1975, emphasised that special education pupils be placed in the last restricted environment, generally meaning in the regular classroom. The regular classroom teacher sometimes has an aide to help care for selected special education pupils in the classroom. There are pupils then in the regular classroom needing much attention and care. All pupils need to receive an education whereby optimal achievement is possible.

There are relevant questions to raise pertaining to mainstreaming pupils:

1. Do some pupils disrupt learning for others so that little achievement is in evidence?
2. Which mainstreamed pupils might receive better instruction in the traditional special education class with a five to one pupil/teacher ration?
3. Are there mainstreamed pupils who are a danger to others especially with a 25 to 1 pupil/teacher ratio in the regular classroom?

Portfolios and Evaluation

There are very strong advocates of using portfolios to appraise pupil achievement. These advocates have been critical of using standardised and criterion referenced test to measure pupil achievement in reading. Standardised tests have no related objectives for teachers to use in teaching pupils. Criterion referenced tests do have specific objectives stated for teachers to use in teaching. The test items on the criterion referenced test measure what pupils have had a chance to learn as indicated in the predetermined precise objectives.

Standardised and criterion referenced test have the same weakness in that educators outside of the local classroom were involving in the developing these tests to ascertain pupil achievement.

Advocates of portfolios believe that pupils should have a voice in how they will be evaluated in the different curriculum areas. Teachers on the local level also desire to have input into appraising their pupils' achievement.

Inside a portfolio, a pupil with teacher guidance determines which snapshots, videotapes, products, processes, and papers will become a part of the former's progress.

Questions that may be asked of portfolio used to appraise pupil achievement include the following:

1. Will portfolios remain as an appropriate way to evaluate pupil achievement, as compared to being a fad?
2. How valid and reliable are portfolios to appraise learner progress?
3. What kind of balance might be available in using both portfolios and tests to appraise pupil achievement.

In Conclusion

Vital issues need to be debated and weaknesses identified. Weaknesses may be modified or deleted. A quality education needs to be in the offing for pupils to achieve. Learning opportunities need to be purposeful, interesting, and meaningful. Evaluation techniques should ascertain pupil achievement. Diagnosis of what pupils are weak in should become objectives for pupils to attain. Vital objectives, only need to be selected for pupils to achieve. Continuous appraisal of the curriculum is a must!

Additional Reading

Bhaskara Rao, Digumarti (1994). *Scientific Aptitude*. New Delhi: Ashish Publishing House. ISBN 81-7024-658-X.

Bhaskara Rao, Digumarti (1995). *Animal Kingdom*. New Delhi: Discovery Publishing House. ISBN 81-7141-274-2.

Bhaskara Rao, Digumarti (1995). *Batracology*. New Delhi: Discovery Publishing House. ISBN 81-7141-279-3.

Bhaskara Rao, Digumarti (1997). *Scientific Attitude*. New Delhi: Discovery Publishing House. ISBN 81-7141-381-1.

Bhaskara Rao, Digumarti (1996). *Scientific Attitude vis-à-vis Scientific Aptitude*. New Delhi: Discovery Publishing House. ISBN 81-7141-308-0.

Bhaskara Rao, Digumarti (2004). *Scientific Attitude, Scientific Aptitude and Achievement*. New Delhi: Discovery Publishing House. ISBN 81-7141-781-7.

Bhaskara Rao, Digumarti (2004). *Educational Administration*. New Delhi: Discovery Publishing House. ISBN 81-7141-842-2.

Bhaskara Rao, Digumarti, editor (1996). *Encyclopaedia of Education For All*, 5 volumes. New Delhi: APH Publishing Corporation. ISBN 81-7024-759-4 (set).

Vol. I *Education For All: The World Conference*. ISBN 81-7024-760-8.

Vol. II *Education For All: The EPA-9 Summit*. ISBN 81-7024-761-6.

Vol. III *Education For All: Quality Education For All.* ISBN 81-7024-762-6.

Vol. IV *Education For All: Planning and Monitoring.* ISBN 81-7024-763-4.

Vol. V *Education For All: The Indian Scenario.* ISBN 81-7024-764-0.

Bhaskara Rao, Digumarti, editor (1996). *Global Perceptions on Peace Education*, 3 volumes. New Delhi: Discovery Publishing House. ISBN 81-7141-319-6.

Bhaskara Rao, Digumarti, editor (1996). *National Policy on Education*, 2 volumes. New Delhi: Anmol Publications Pvt. Ltd. ISBN 81-7488-323-1.

Bhaskara Rao, Digumarti, editor (1997). *Care the Child*, 2 volumes. New Delhi: Discovery Publishing House. ISBN 81-7141-394-3.

Bhaskara Rao, Digumarti, editor (1997). *Education for the 21st Century*. New Delhi: Discovery Publishing House. ISBN 81-7141-389-7.

Bhaskara Rao, Digumarti, editor (1997). *Reflections on Scientific Attitude*. New Delhi: Discovery Publishing House. ISBN 81-7141-319-6.

Bhaskara Rao, Digumarti, editor (1997). *Success Story of a Primary Education Project*. New Delhi: APH Publishing Corporation. ISBN 81-7024-850-7.

Bhaskara Rao, Digumarti, editor (1997). *World Food Summit*. New Delhi: Discovery Publishing House. ISBN 81-7141-386-2.

Bhaskara Rao, Digumarti, editor (1998). *Adolescence Education*. New Delhi: Discovery Publishing House. ISBN 81-7141-432-X.

Bhaskara Rao, Digumarti, editor (1998). *Community and School Nutrition Education*. New Delhi: Discovery Publishing House. ISBN 81-7141-435-4.

Bhaskara Rao, Digumarti, editor (1998). *District Primary Education Programme*. New Delhi: Discovery Publishing House. ISBN 81-7141-396-X.

Bhaskara Rao, Digumarti, editor (1998). *Earth Summit*, 2 volumes. New Delhi: Discovery Publishing House. ISBN 81-7141-435-4.

Bhaskara Rao, Digumarti, editor (1998). *National Policy on Education: Towards an Enlightened and Humane Society*. New Delhi: Discovery Publishing House. ISBN 81-7141-426-5.

Bhaskara Rao, Digumarti, editor (1998). *Reforming School Education*. New Delhi: Discovery Publishing House. ISBN 81-7141-403-6.

Bhaskara Rao, Digumarti, editor (1998). *Teacher Education in India*. New Delhi: Discovery Publishing House. ISBN 81-7141-406-0.

Bhaskara Rao, Digumarti, editor (1998). *World Summit for Social Development*. New Delhi: Discovery Publishing House. ISBN 81-7141-420-6.

Bhaskara Rao, Digumarti, editor (2000). *Education For All: Achieving the Goal*, 3 volumes. New Delhi: APH Publishing Corporation. ISBN 81-7648-152-1 (set).

Vol. I *The Global Consensus*. ISBN 81-7648-155-6.

Vol. II *Mid-Decade Review Reports of Regional Seminars*. ISBN 81-7648-154-8.

Vol. III *Issues and Trends*. ISBN 81-7648-155-6.

Bhaskara Rao, Digumarti, editor (1999). *International Encyclopaedia of AIDS*, 11 volumes. New Delhi: Discovery Publishing House. ISBN 81-7141-522-6 (set).

Vol. 1 *Introduction to HIV/AIDS*. ISBN 81-7141-523-7.

Vol. 2 *HIV/AIDS-Issues and Challenges*, 2 parts. ISBN 81-7141-524-5.

Vol. 3 *HIV/AIDS-Socio Economic Realities*. ISBN 81-7141-524-3.

Vol. 4 *HIV/AIDS-Law Ethics and Human Rights*, 2 parts. ISBN 81-7141-526-1.

Vol. 5 *AIDS and NGOs*. ISBN 81-7141-527-X.

Vol. 6 *AIDS and Home Care*. ISBN 81-7141-528-8.

Vol. 7 *STD Case Management*. ISBN 81-7141-529-6.

Vol. 8 *HIV/AIDS Prevention and Care-Teaching Modules for Nurses and Midwives*. ISBN 81-7141-530-X.

Vol. 9 *HIV Prevention Education for Educational Institutions*. ISBN 81-7141-531-8.

Vol.10 *Instructional Modules for AIDS Education*. ISBN 81-7141-532-6.

Vol.11 *School Health Education to prevent AIDS and STD-A Package for Curriculum Planners*. ISBN 81-7141-533-4.

Bhaskara Rao, Digumarti, editor (2000). *International Encyclopaedia of Science and Technology Education*, 11 volumes. New Delhi: Discovery Publishing House. ISBN 81-7141-548-2 (set).

Vol. 1 *Science and Technology Education*. ISBN 81-7141-568-7.

Vol. 2 *Science Education in Developing Countries*. ISBN 81-7141-569-9.

Vol. 3 *Organizational Structure of Science*. ISBN 81-7141-570-9.

Vol. 4 *Science Education in Asia and the Pacific*. ISBN 81-7141-571-7

Vol. 5 *Science and Technology Education For All*. ISBN 81-7141-572-5.

Vol. 6 *Values, Ethics, Talent and Girls in Science and Technology Education*. ISBN 81-7141-573-3.

Vol. 7 *Popularization of Science and Technology Education*. ISBN.81-7141-574-1.

Vol. 8 *Science, Power and Society*. ISBN 81-7141-575-X.

Vol. 9 *Information Technology*. ISBN 81-7141-576-8.

Vol. 10 *Teacher Training in Science and Technology Education*. ISBN 81-7142-577-6.

Vol. 11 *Teacher Training in Science and Technology: A Curriculum Framework*. ISBN 81-7141-578-4.

Bhaskara Rao, Digumarti, editor (2001). *Distance Education in Different Countries*. New Delhi: APH Publishing Corporation. ISBN 81-7648-229-3.

Bhaskara Rao, Digumarti, editor (2001). *Decentralised Management of Education: Management of Education in Panchayati Raj and Municipal Bodies*. New Delhi: Discovery Publishing House. ISBN 81-7141-617-9.

Bhaskara Rao, Digumarti, editor (2001). *Electrochemistry for Environmental Protection*. New Delhi: Discovery Publishing House. ISBN 81-7141-619-5.

Bhaskara Rao, Digumarti, editor (2001). *Global Educational Studies*. New Delhi: Discovery Publishing House. ISBN 81-7141-616-0.

Bhaskara Rao, Digumarti, editor (2001). *Global Synthesis of Educational Assessment*. New Delhi: Discovery Publishing House. ISBN 81-7141-613-6.

Bhaskara Rao, Digumarti, editor (2000). *International Encyclopaedia of Human Rights*, 7 volumes in 13 parts. New Delhi: Discovery Publishing House. ISBN 81-7141-567-9 (set).

Vol. 1 *International Instruments of Human Rights*, 2 parts. ISBN 81-7141-569-4.

Vol. 2 *Regional Instruments of Human Rights*. ISBN 81-7141-604-7.

Vol. 3 *Human Rights and the United Nations*, 2 parts. ISBN 81-7141-605-5.

Vol. 4 *Fact Files of Human Rights*, 3 parts. ISBN 81-7141-606-3.

Vol. 5 *Study Stories of Human Rights*, 3 parts. ISBN 81-7141-607-3.

Vol. 6 *International Meetings on Human Rights*, 2 parts.ISBN 81-714-608-X.

Vol. 7 *Professional Training in Human Rights.* ISBN 81-7141-609-8.

Bhaskara Rao, Digumarti, editor (2001). *Jomtein Decade of Education.* New Delhi: Discovery Publishing House. ISBN 81-7141-618-7.

Bhaskara Rao, Digumarti, editor (2001). *Nuclear Materials: Issues and Concerns*, 2 volumes. New Delhi: Discovery Publishing House. ISBN 81-7141-611-X.

Bhaskara Rao, Digumarti, editor (2001). *World Conference on Education for All.* New Delhi: APH Publishing Corporation. ISBN 81-7141-274-9.

Bhaskara Rao, Digumarti, editor (2001). *World Conference on Higher Education.* New Delhi: Discovery Publishing House. ISBN 81-7141-610-1.

Bhaskara Rao, Digumarti, editor (2001). *World Conference on Science.* New Delhi: Discovery Publishing House. ISBN 81-7141-612-8.

Bhaskara Rao, Digumarti, editor (2003). *Inspiring Experiences in Teacher Education.* New Delhi: Discovery Publishing House. ISBN 81-7141-656-X.

Bhaskara Rao, Digumarti, editor (2003). *International Studies in Education*, 3 volumes. New Delhi: Discovery Publishing House. ISBN 81-7141-647-0.

Bhaskara Rao, Digumarti, editor (2003). *Military Conversion: Impact on Science and Technology.* New Delhi: Discovery Publishing House. ISBN 81-7141-578-4.

Bhaskara Rao, Digumarti, editor (2003). *United Nations Millennium Summit.* New Delhi: Discovery Publishing House. ISBN 81-7141-632-2.

Bhaskara Rao, Digumarti, editor (2003). *World Assembly on Aging. New Delhi*: Discovery Publishing House. ISBN 81-7141-637-3.

Bhaskara Rao, Digumarti, editor (2003). *World Conference on Human Rights.* New Delhi: Discovery Publishing House. ISBN 81-7141-661-6.

Bhaskara Rao, Digumarti, editor (2003). *World Education Forum*. New Delhi: Discovery Publishing House. ISBN 81-7141-639-X.

Bhaskara Rao, Digumarti, editor (2003). *Education, Employment and Human Resource Development*. New Delhi: Discovery Publishing House. ISBN 81-7141-681-0.

Bhaskara Rao, Digumarti, editor (2003). *Successful Schooling*. New Delhi: Discovery Publishing House. ISBN 81-7141-677-2.

Bhaskara Rao, Digumarti, editor (2003). *European Education and Teachers*. New Delhi: Discovery Publishing House. ISBN 81-7141-702-7.

Bhaskara Rao, Digumarti, editor (2003). *Teachers in a Changing World*. New Delhi: Discovery Publishing House. ISBN 81-7141-694-2.

Bhaskara Rao, Digumarti, editor (2004). *International Encyclopaedia of Learning to Live Together*, 4 volumes. New Delhi: Discovery Publishing House. ISBN 81-7141-848-1.

Vol. 1 *International Conference on Learning to Live Together.*

Vol. 2 *Globalization and Living Together.*

Vol. 3 *Curriculum for Learning to Live Together.*

Vol. 4 *Science Education for the Contemporary Society.*

Bhaskara Rao, Digumarti, editor (2004). *International Guidelines on Open and Distance Teacher Education*. New Delhi: Discovery Publishing House. ISBN 81-7141-777-9.

Bhaskara Rao, Digumarti, editor (2004). *Adult Learning in the 21st Century*. New Delhi: Discovery Publishing House. ISBN 81-7141-797-3.

Bhaskara Rao, Digumarti, editor (2004). *Educational Practices: Research and Recommendations*. New Delhi: Discovery Publishing House. ISBN 81-7141-835-X.

—

Bhaskara Rao, Digumarti, editor (2004). *General Secondary Education In the 21st Century*. New Delhi: Discovery Publishing House. ISBN 81-7141-885-6.

Bhaskara Rao, Digumarti, editor (2004). *Reforming Secondary Education*. New Delhi: Discovery Publishing House. ISBN 81-7141-843-0.

Bhaskara Rao, Digumarti, editor (2004). *Human Rights Education*. New Delhi: Discovery Publishing House. ISBN 81-7141-882-1.

Bhaskara Rao, Digumarti, editor (2004). *United Nations Decade for Human Rights Education*. New Delhi: Discovery Publishing House. ISBN 81-7141-887-2.

Bhaskara Rao, Digumarti and B.S.V. Dutt, editors (2003). *Education: Programmes and Policies*. New Delhi: APH Publishing Corporation. ISBN 81-7648-470-9.

Bhaskara Rao, Digumarti, C.A.P. Swamy and B.S.V. Dutt (1997). *Self-Evaluation in Student Teaching*. New Delhi: Discovery Publishing House. ISBN 81-7141-374-9.

Bhaskara Rao, Digumarti and D. Naresh Kumar (2004). *School Teacher Effectiveness*. New Delhi: Discovery Publishing House. ISBN 81-7141-782-5.

Bhaskara Rao, Digumarti and D. Sridhar (2002). *Job Satisfaction of School Teachers*. New Delhi: Discovery Publishing House. ISBN 81-7141-652-7.

Bhaskara Rao, Digumarti, C. Sridevi and K. Vijaya (1995). *Achievement in Social Studies*. New Delhi: Discovery Publishing House. ISBN 81-7141-281-5.

Bhaskara Rao, Digumarti and Digumarti Pushpa Latha (1994). *Achievement in Biology*. New Delhi: Discovery Publishing House. ISBN 81-7141-264-5.

Bhaskara Rao, Digumarti and Digumarti Pushpa Latha (1995). *Achievement in English*. New Delhi: Discovery Publishing House. ISBN 81-7141-283-1.

Bhaskara Rao, Digumarti and Digumarti Pushpa Latha (1994). *Achievement in Science*. New Delhi: Discovery Publishing House. ISBN 81-7141-280-70.

Bhaskara Rao, Digumarti and Digumarti Pushpa Latha (1995). *Achievement in Mathematics*. New Delhi: Discovery Publishing House. ISBN 81-7141-278-5.

Bhaskara Rao, Digumarti and Digumarti Pushpa Latha (2004). *Education for Women*. New Delhi: Discovery Publishing House. ISBN 81-7141-873-2.

Bhaskara Rao, Digumarti and Digumarti Pushpa Latha, editors (1998). *International Encyclopaedia of Women*, 5 volumes. New Delhi: Discovery Publishing House. ISBN 81-7141-410-9 (set).

Vol. 1 *Status of World's Women*. ISBN 81-7141-494-X.

Vol. 2 *Women, Education and Empowerment*. ISBN 81-7141-498-1.

Vol. 3 *Women Challenges and Advancement*. ISBN 81-7141-497-4.

Vol. 4 *Women and Family Health*. ISBN 81-7141-497-4.

Vol. 5 *Women and International Action*. ISBN 81-7141-498-2.

Bhaskara Rao, Digumarti, Digumarti Pushpa Latha and Digumarthi Harshitha, editors (2001). *Biological Warfare*. New Delhi: Discovery Publishing House. ISBN 81-7141-597-0.

Bhaskara Rao, Digumarti, Digumarti Pushpa Latha and Digumarthi Harshitha, editors (2001). *Women as Educators*. New Delhi: Discovery Publishing House. ISBN 81-7141-602-0.

Bhaskara Rao, Digumarti and Digumarthi Harshitha (2004). *Adjustment of Adolescents*. New Delhi: APH Publishing House. ISBN 81-7648-836-8.

Bhaskara Rao, Digumarti and Digumarthi Harshitha, editors (2001). *Education in India*. New Delhi: APH Publishing House. ISBN 81-7648-207-2.

Bhaskara Rao, Digumarti, Digumarti Pushpa Latha and Digumarthi Harshitha, editors (2001). *Assessing Learning Achievement*. New Delhi: Discovery Publishing House. ISBN 81-7141-601-2.

Bhaskara Rao, Digumarti, Digumarti Pushpa Latha and Digumarthi Harshitha, editors (2001). *Energy Security*. New Delhi: Discovery Publishing House. ISBN 81-7141-598-9.

Bhaskara Rao, Digumarti, Digumarthi Harshitha and K.R.S. Sambasiva Rao, editors (1999). *Advanced Biotechnology*. New Delhi: Discovery Publishing House. ISBN 81-7141-516-4.

Bhaskara Rao, Digumarti and K.R.S.Sambasiva Rao, editors (1996). *Current Trends in Indian Education*. New Delhi: Discovery Publishing House. ISBN 81-7141-311-0.

Bhaskara Rao, Digumarti and D. Naresh Kumar (2004). *School Teacher Effectiveness*. New Delhi: Discovery Publishing House. ISBN 81-7141-782-5.

Bhaskara Rao, Digumarti and E. Sreekanth Babu (2004). *Educational Interests of School Students*. New Delhi: Discovery Publishing House. ISBN 81-7141-837-6.

Bhaskara Rao, Digumarti and K. Vijaya (1995). *A Text Book Evaluation*. Ambala Cantt: The Associated Publishers.

Bhaskara Rao, Digumarti and M.A. Fayaz (2004). *Problems of Primary School Drop-outs*. New Delhi: Discovery Publishing House. ISBN 81-7141-834-1.

Bhaskara Rao, Digumarti and N.V.M. Mohana Rao (2002). *Problems of Mentally Handicapped Children*. New Delhi: Discovery Publishing House. ISBN 81-7141-645-4.

Bhaskara Rao, Digumarti and S. Chandra Mohan (2002). *Sports Management*. New Delhi: APH Publishing House. ISBN 81-7648-467-9.

Bhaskara Rao, Digumarti and S.A. Khader (2004). *Problems of Private School Teachers*. New Delhi: Discovery Publishing Corporation. ISBN 81-7141-838-4.

Bhaskara Rao, Digumarti and S.A. Khader (2004). *School Education in India*. New Delhi: Discovery Publishing Corporation. ISBN 81-7141-849-X.

Bhaskara Rao, Digumarti and Sk. Johni Basha (2004). *Teachers' Population Education Awareness*. New Delhi: Discovery Publishing House. ISBN 81-7141-832-5.

Bhaskara Rao, Digumarti, V.V. Rao, V.V. Lakshmi and V.V. Krishna, editors (1999). *Status and Advancement of Women*. New Delhi: APH Publishing Corporation. ISBN 81-7648-169-6.

Babu, P.C., author and Digumarti Bhaskara Rao, editor (2004). *Flowers of Wisdom*. New Delhi: Discovery Publishing House. ISBN 81-7141-695-0.

Amala, P.A. and Anupam, P., authors and Digumarti Bhaskara Rao, editor (2004). *History of Education*. New Delhi: Discovery Publishing House. ISBN 81-7141-860-0.

Bhagya Lakshmi, L., author and Digumarti Bhaskara Rao, editor (2000). *Reading and Comprehension*. New Delhi: Discovery Publishing House. ISBN 81-7141-543-1.

Bhasha, S.A., author and Digumarti Bhaskara Rao, editor (2004). *Methods of Teaching Geography*. New Delhi: Discovery Publishing House. ISBN 81-7141-807-4.

Bhuvaneswara Lakshmi, Gadde, author and Digumarti Bhaskara Rao, editor (2000). *Attitude Towards Science*. New Delhi: Discovery Publishing House. ISBN 81-7141-541-6.

Bhuvaneswari Lakshmi, G., author and Digumarti Bhaskara Rao, editor (2004). *Methods of Teaching Life Science*. New Delhi: Discovery Publishing House. ISBN 81-7141-804-X.

Bhuvaneswari Lakshmi, G. and K. Subba Rao, authors and Digumarti Bhaskara Rao, editor (2004). *Methods of Teaching Biology*. New Delhi: Discovery Publishing House. ISBN 81-7141-914-3.

Chowdary, S.B.J.R. and Naga Raju authors and Digumarti Bhaskara Rao, editor (2004). *Mastery of Teaching Skills*. New Delhi: Discovery Publishing House. ISBN 81-7141-861-9.

Devraj, T.A.S., author and Digumarti Bhaskara Rao, editor (1997). *Trace Analysis of Uranium and Thorium*. New Delhi: Discovery Publishing House. ISBN 81-7141-375-7.

Durga Rani, K., author and Digumarti Bhaskara Rao, editor (2000). *Educational Aspirations and Scientific Attitudes*. New Delhi: Discovery Publishing House. ISBN 81-7141-555-5.

Dutt, B.S.V. and Digumarti Bhaskara Rao (2001). *Empowering Primary Teachers*. New Delhi: Discovery Publishing House. ISBN 81-7141-615-2.

Dutt, B.S.V., author and Digumarti Bhaskara Rao, editor (2004). *Comparative Education*. New Delhi: Discovery Publishing House. ISBN 81-7141-912-7.

Ediger, Marlow and Digumarti Bhaskara Rao (1996). *Science Curriculum*. New Delhi: Discovery Publishing House. ISBN 81-7141-321-8.

Ediger, Marlow and Digumarti Bhaskara Rao (2000). *Teaching Mathematics Successfully*. New Delhi: Discovery Publishing House. ISBN 81-7141-552-0.

Ediger, Marlow and Digumarti Bhaskara Rao (2001). *Teaching Science Successfully*. New Delhi: Discovery Publishing House. ISBN 81-7141-600-4.

Ediger, Marlow and Digumarti Bhaskara Rao (2001). *Teaching Social Studies Successfully*. New Delhi: Discovery Publishing House. ISBN 81-7141-596-2.

Ediger, Marlow and Digumarti Bhaskara Rao (2002). *Philosophy and Curriculum*. New Delhi: Discovery Publishing House. ISBN 81-7141-631-4.

Ediger, Marlow and Digumarti Bhaskara Rao (2002). *Improving School Administration*. New Delhi: Discovery Publishing House. ISBN 81-7141-633-0.

Ediger, Marlow and Digumarti Bhaskara Rao (2002). *Elementary Curriculum*. New Delhi: Discovery Publishing House. ISBN 81-7141-658-6.

Ediger, Marlow and Digumarti Bhaskara Rao (2003). *Language Arts Curriculum*. New Delhi: Discovery Publishing House. ISBN 81-7141-657-8.

Ediger, Marlow and Digumarti Bhaskara Rao (2003). *Psychology and Curriculum*. New Delhi: Discovery Publishing House. ISBN 81-7141-691-8.

Ediger, Marlow and Digumarti Bhaskara Rao (2003). *Teaching Language Arts Successfully*. New Delhi: Discovery Publishing House. ISBN 81-7141-678-0.

Ediger, Marlow and Digumarti Bhaskara Rao (2003). *School Curriculum and Administration*. New Delhi: Discovery Publishing House. ISBN 81-7141-709-4.

Ediger, Marlow and Digumarti Bhaskara Rao (2003). *Teaching Mathematics in Elementary Schools*. New Delhi: Discovery Publishing House. ISBN 81-7141-687-X.

Ediger, Marlow and Digumarti Bhaskara Rao (2003). Teaching Science in Elementary Schools. New Delhi: Discovery Publishing House. ISBN 81-7141-698-5.

Ediger, Marlow and Digumarti Bhaskara Rao (2003). *School Curriculum and Administration*. New Delhi: Discovery Publishing House. ISBN 81-7141-709-4.

Ediger, Marlow and Digumarti Bhaskara Rao (2003). *Elementary Curriculum Improvement*. New Delhi: Discovery Publishing House. ISBN 81-7141-740-X.

Ediger, Marlow and Digumarti Bhaskara Rao (2004). *School Organisation*. New Delhi: Discovery Publishing House. ISBN 81-7141-843-0.

Ediger, Marlow and Digumarti Bhaskara Rao (2004). *Relevancy in Elementary Curriculum*. New Delhi: Discovery Publishing House. ISBN 81-7141-845-9.

Ediger, Marlow, B.S.V. Dutt and Digumarti Bhaskara Rao (2003). *Teaching English Successfully*. New Delhi: Discovery Publishing House. ISBN 81-7141-707-8.

Elizabeth, M.E.S., author and Digumarti Bhaskara Rao, editor (2004). *Methods of Teaching English*. New Delhi: Discovery Publishing House. ISBN 81-7141-809-0.

Harshitha, D. author and Digumarti Bhaskara Rao, editor (2004). *Methods of Teaching Information Technology*. New Delhi: Discovery Publishing House. ISBN 81-7141-805-8.

Indira Devi, author and J. Prasanth Kumar and Digumarti Bhaskara Rao, editors (2004). *Values in Language Text Books*. New Delhi: APH Publishing Corporation. ISBN 81-7141-833-3.

Jalaja Kumari, C., author and Digumarti Bhaskara Rao, editor (2004). *Methods of Teaching Educational Technology*. New Delhi: Discovery Publishing House. ISBN 81-7141-810-4.

Jayasree, Kandi, author and Digumarti Bhaskara Rao, editor (1999). *Correlates of Socialisation*. New Delhi: Discovery Publishing House. ISBN 81-7141-517-2.

Jayasree, Kandi, author and Digumarti Bhaskara Rao, editor (2004). *Methods of Teaching Science*. New Delhi: Discovery Publishing House. ISBN 81-7141-801-5.

John Babu, Chikati, author and T.J.R. Prasad, G.M. Madhukar and Digumarti Bhaskara Rao, editors (1996). *Problem Solving in Mathematics*. New Delhi: APH Publishing Corporation. ISBN 81-7648-273-0.

Joseph Raju, B and G.A. Anitha, authors and Digumarti Bhaskara Rao, editor (2004). *Population Education*. New Delhi: Sonali Publications. ISBN 81-88836-31-3.

Lalitha, T., author and K.S. Prabhakaram, D.S.N. Sastry and Digumarti Bhaskara Rao, editors (2004). *Educational Philosophic Beliefs*. New Delhi: Discovery Publishing House. ISBN 81-7141-765-5.

Madhu Bala, Jampala, author and Digumarti Bhaskara Rao, editor (2004). *Adjustment Problems of Hearing Impaired*. New Delhi: Discovery Publishing House. ISBN 81-7141-831-7.

Madhu Bala, Jampala, author and Digumarti Bhaskara Rao, editor (2004). *Methods of Teaching Exceptional Children*. New Delhi: Discovery Publishing House. ISBN 81-7141-802-3.

Marja, Talvi and Digumarti Bhaskara Rao, editors (1996). *Educational Leadership and Social Changes*. New Delhi: Discovery Publishing House. ISBN 81-7141-320-X.

Nageswara Rao, S.and M. Srihari, authors and Digumarti Bhaskara Rao, editor (2004). *Guidance and Counselling*. New Delhi: Discovery Publishing House. ISBN 81-7141-840-6.

Nageswara Rao, S. and P. Sridhar, authors and Digumarti Bhaskara Rao, editor (2004). *Methods and Techniques of Teaching*. New Delhi: Sonali Publications. ISBN 81-88836-33-8.

Nirmala Jyothi, M., author and Digumarti Bhaskara Rao, editor (2003). *Non-detention System in School Education*. New Delhi: Discovery Publishing House. ISBN 81-7141-654-3.

Padma Tulasi, G., author and Digumarti Bhaskara Rao, editor (2004). *Methods of Teaching Elementary Science*. New Delhi: Discovery Publishing House. ISBN 81-7141-871-6.

Pala Prasada Rao, V., author and K. Nirupa Rani and Digumarti Bhaskara Rao, editors (2004). *Methods of Teaching Elementary Science*. New Delhi: Discovery Publishing House. ISBN 81-7141-871-6.

Prabhakaram, K.S., author and Digumarti Bhaskara Rao, editors (1998). *Concept Attainment Model in Mathematics Teaching*. New Delhi: Discovery Publishing House. ISBN 81-7141-424-9.

Prasanth Kumar, J., author and Digumarti Bhaskara Rao, editor (1998). *Effectiveness of Distance Education System*. New Delhi: Discovery Publishing House. ISBN 81-7141-437-0.

Prasanth Kumar, J., author and Digumarti Bhaskara Rao, editor (2004). *Methods of Teaching Civics*. New Delhi: Discovery Publishing House. ISBN 81-7141-806-6.

Prasanth Kumar, J., author and G. Sundara Rao and Digumarti Bhaskara Rao, editors (2000). *Open University Student Support Services*. New Delhi: Discovery Publishing House. ISBN 81-7141-550-4.

Raja Kumari, M.A. and D.R.S. Sundari, authors and Digumarti Bhaskara Rao, editor (2004). *Special Education*. New Delhi: Discovery Publishing House. ISBN 81-7141-846-5.

Raja Kumari, M.A. and D.R.S. Sundari, authors and Digumarti Bhaskara Rao, editor (2004). *Methods of Teaching Educational Psychology*. New Delhi: Discovery Publishing House. ISBN 81-7141-820-1.

Ramatulasamma, K., author and Digumarti Bhaskara Rao, editor (2002). *Job Satisfaction of Teacher Educators*. New Delhi: Discovery Publishing House. ISBN 81-7141-655-1.

Rama Krishnaiah, D., author and Digumarti Bhaskara Rao, editor (1998). *Job Satisfaction of College Teachers*. New Delhi: Discovery Publishing House. ISBN 81-7141-438-9.

Rama Kumar Ratnam, M.V., author and Digumarti Bhaskara Rao, editor (1998). *Dukkha: Suffering in Early Buddhism*. New Delhi: Discovery Publishing House. ISBN 81-7141-653-5.

Rama Krishna Prasad and P. Vide Sagar, authors and Digumarti Bhaskara Rao, editor (2004). *Methods of Teaching Physical Education*. New Delhi: Discovery Publishing House. ISBN 81-7141-868-6.

Rama Seshaiah, P. author and Digumarti Bhaskara Rao, editor (2004). *Methods of Teaching Home Science*. New Delhi: Discovery Publishing House. ISBN 81-7141-916-X.

Ramesh, Ganta and Digumarti Bhaskara Rao, editors (1998). *Environmental Education: Problems and Prospects*. New Delhi: Discovery Publishing House. ISBN 81-7141-423-0.

Ranga Rao, R., author and Digumarti Bhaskara Rao, editor (2004). *Methods of Teacher Teaching*. New Delhi: Discovery Publishing House. ISBN 81-7141-812-0.

Rathaiah, Lavu and Digumarti Bhaskara Rao, editors (1996), *International Innovations in Education*. New Delhi: Discovery Publishing House. ISBN 81-7141-359-5.

Rathaiah, Lavu and Digumarti Bhaskara Rao (1997). *Achievement Correlates*. New Delhi: Discovery Publishing House. ISBN 81-7141-385-4.

Ravi Krishna, M., author and Digumarti Bhaskara Rao, editor (2004). *Examination System*. New Delhi: Discovery Publishing House. ISBN 81-7141-824-4.

Ravi Kumar, M., author and Digumarti Bhaskara Rao, editor (2004). *Methods of Teaching Computer Science*. New Delhi: Discovery Publishing House. ISBN 81-7141-823-6.

Reddy, Sudhakar Y., author and Digumarti Bhaskara Rao, editor (2003). *Creativity in Adolescents*. New Delhi: Discovery Publishing House. ISBN 81-7141-659-4.

Reddy, M. S., author and Digumarti Bhaskara Rao, editor (2004). *Creativity in College Students*. New Delhi: Discovery Publishing House. ISBN 81-7141-697-7.

Rudramamba, B., author and Digumarti Bhaskara Rao, editor (2003). *Problems of Teaching*. New Delhi: APH Publishing Corporation. ISBN 81-7648-462-8.

Rudramamba, B. and V. Lakshmi Kumari, authors and Digumarti Bhaskara Rao, editor (2004). *Methods of Teaching Economics*. New Delhi: Discovery Publishing House. ISBN 81-7141-900-3.

Sanjeeva Rao, P.C., author and Digumarti Bhaskara Rao, editor (1996). *A Text Book of Geology*. New Delhi: Discovery Publishing House. ISBN 81-7141-313-7.

Satya Narayana, V., author and Digumarti Bhaskara Rao, editor (2001). *Physical Education, Social Attitudes and Leadership Qualities*. New Delhi: Discovery Publishing House. ISBN 81-7141-593-8.

Satya Narayana, P.V.V. and G. Krishna, authors and Digumarti Bhaskara Rao, editor (2004). *Curriculum Development and Management*. New Delhi: Discovery Publishing House. ISBN 81-7141-813-9.

Siva Lakshmi, G.V. and G.L. Subbaiah, authors and Digumarti Bhaskara Rao, editor (2004). *Methods of Teaching Environmental Science*. New Delhi: Discovery Publishing House. ISBN 81-7141-839-2.

Srinivas, M. and I. Prasada Rao, authors and Digumarti Bhaskara Rao, editor (2004). *Methods of Teaching History*. New Delhi: Discovery Publishing House. ISBN 81-7141-803-1.

Srinivasulu Reddy, M. and K.R.S. Sambasiva Rao, authors and Digumarti Bhaskara Rao, editor (1999). *A Text Book of Aquaculture*. New Delhi: Discovery Publishing House. ISBN 81-7141-482-6.

Srinivasa Rao, Mandalapu, author and Digumarti Bhaskara Rao, editor (2003). *Achievement Motivation and Achievement in Mathematics*. New Delhi: Discovery Publishing House. ISBN 81-7141-674-8.

Sunil Kumar, K. and K. Rama Krishana, authors and Digumarti Bhaskara Rao, editor (2004). *Methods of Teaching Chemistry*. New Delhi: Discovery Publishing House. ISBN 81-7141-913-5.

Sunita, E. and R. Sambasiva Rao, authors and Digumarti Bhaskara Rao, editor (2004). *Methods of Teaching Mathematics*. New Delhi: Discovery Publishing House. ISBN 81-7141-915-1.

Swarupa Rani, T. and J.R. Priyadarshini, authors and Digumarti Bhaskara Rao, editor (2004). *Educational Measurement and Evaluation*. New Delhi: Discovery Publishing House. ISBN 81-7141-859-7.

Vanaja, M., author and Digumarti Bhaskara Rao, editor (1999). *Inquiry Training Model*. New Delhi: Discovery Publishing House. ISBN 81-7141-515-6.

Vanaja,M., author and Digumarti Bhaskara Rao, editor (2004). *Methods of Teaching Physics*. New Delhi: Discovery Publishing House. ISBN 81-7141-867-8

Valeri V. Koustiouk, author and Digumarti Bhaskara Rao, editor (2002). *A Text Book of Cryogenics*. New Delhi: Discovery Publishing House. ISBN 81-7141-642-X.

Vamsi Krishana, V., author and Digumarti Bhaskara Rao, editor (2004). *School Psychology*. New Delhi: Discovery Publishing House. ISBN 81-7141-880-5.

Veena Kumari, Balusu and Digumarti Bhaskara Rao (1996). *Operation Black Board*. New Delhi: APH Publishing Corporation. ISBN 81-7024-711-X.

Veena Kumari, B. author and Digumarti Bhaskara Rao, editor (2004). *Methods of Teaching Social Studies*. New Delhi: Discovery Publishing House. ISBN 81-7141-899-6.

Veena Kumari, Balusu, author and Digumarti Bhaskara Rao, editor (2000). *Psycho-Social Correlates of Achievement*. New Delhi: Discovery Publishing House. ISBN 81-7141-547-4.

Venkata Rao, P. and Digumarti Bhaskara Rao (1989). *A Text Book of Zoology-Junior Intermediate*. Guntur: Vignan Publishers.

Venkata Rao, P. and Digumarti Bhaskara Rao (1989). *A Text Book of Zoology-Senior Intermediate*. Guntur: Vignan Publishers.

Venkateswara Reddy, L. and Lakshmi Narayana, M., authors and Digumarti Bhaskara Rao, editor (2004). *Methods of Teaching Rural Sociology*. New Delhi: Discovery Publishing House. ISBN 81-7141-811-2.

Venkateswara Rao, V., author and Digumarti Bhaskara Rao, editor (2004). *Problems of Education*. New Delhi: Discovery Publishing House. ISBN 81-7141-841-4.

Venkateswara Rao, V., V. Vijaya Lakshmi and V. Vamsi Krishna, authors and Digumarti Bhaskara Rao, editor (2004). *Education For All*. New Delhi: Sonali Publications. ISBN 81-88836-30-3.

Venkateswara Rao, V., V. Vijaya Lakshmi and V. Vamsi Krishna, authors and Digumarti Bhaskara Rao, editor (2004). *Education in India*. New Delhi: Sonali Publications. ISBN 81-88836-858-9.

Venkateswara Reddy, L. and Lakshmi Narayana, M., authors and Digumarti Bhaskara Rao, editor (2004). *Education for Dalits*. New Delhi: Discovery Publishing House. ISBN 81-7141-872-4.

Venkateswarlu, K. and S.J. Basha, authors and Digumarti Bhaskara Rao, editor (2004). *Methods of Teaching Commerce*. New Delhi: Discovery Publishing House. ISBN 81-7141-808-2.

Venugopala Rao, K., author and Digumarti Bhaskara Rao, editor (2000). *Teacher Morale in Secondary Schools*. New Delhi: Discovery Publishing House. ISBN 81-7141-551-2.

Vidya, C., author and Digumarti Bhaskara Rao, editor (1996). *A Text Book of Nutrition*. New Delhi: Discovery Publishing House. ISBN 81-7141-309-9.

Vijaya Bharathi, D., author and Digumarti Bhaskara Rao, editor (2000). *Educational Philosophies of Swami Vivekananda and John Dewey*. New Delhi: APH Publishing House. ISBN 81-7648-309-9.

Vijaya Lakshmi, D., author and Digumarti Bhaskara Rao, editor (2004) *Basic Education*. New Delhi: Discovery Publishing House. ISBN 81-7141-881-3.

Books in Telugu Language

Bhaskara Rao, Digumarti (1986). *Dhrushya Sravana Bodhanapakaranalu (Audio Visual Teaching Aids)*. Guntur: Nagarjuna Publishers.

Bhaskara Rao, Digumarti (1993). *Jeevasashtra Bodhana (Teaching of Biology)*. Guntur: Nagarjuna Publishers.

Bhaskara Rao, Digumarti (1995). *Vignanasasthra Bodhana (Teaching of science)* Guntur: Nagarjuna Publishers.

Bhaskara Rao, Digumarti (1997). *Vidya Manovignana Seshtram (Educational Psychology)*. Guntur: Creative Press.

Bhaskara Rao, Digumarti (1998). *DSC Study Material*. Guntur: Nagarjuna Publishers.

Bhaskara Rao, Digumarti (1998). *Upadhyayudu Vidya. (Teacher and Education)* Guntur: Nagarjuna Publishers.

Bhaskara Rao, Digumarti (1998). *Vidya Drukpadalu (Perspectives of Education)*. Guntur: Nagarjuna Publishers.

Bhaskara Rao, Digumarti (1999). *EdCET Teaching Aptitude*. Guntur: Nagarjuna Publishers.

Bhaskara Rao, Digumarti (2001). *Bharata Samajamulo Upadyayudu Vidya (Teacher and Education in Emerging Indian Society)*. Guntur: Sri Nagarjuna Publishers.

Bhaskara Rao, Digumarti (2001). *Bhoutika Sastra Bodhana Paddathulu (Methods of Teaching Physical Science)*. Guntur: Sri Nagarjuna Publishers.

Bhaskara Rao, Digumarti (2001). *Jeeva Sastra Bodhana Padhathulu (Methods of Teaching Biology)*. Guntur: Sri Nagarjuna Publishers.

Bhaskara Rao, Digumarti (2001). *Vidya Manovignana Sastram (Educational Psychology)*. Guntur: Sri Nagarjuna Publishers.

Bhaskara Rao, Digumarti (2003). *Patasula Yajamanyam / Paripalana (School Management and Administration)*. Guntur: Sri Nagarjuna Publishers.

Gopala Krishna, G., A. Ramkrishna, K. Subba Rao and Bhaskara Rao, Digumarti (2004). *Jeevasashtra Bodhana Padhatulu (Methods of Teaching of Biological science)*. Guntur: Sri Nagarjuna Publishers.

Krishna Murthy, V., K.S. Sudheer Reddy and Digumarti Bhaskara Rao (2004). *Vidya Manovignana Sastra Adharalu (Foundations of Educational Psychology)*. Guntur: Sri Nagarjuna Publishers.

Lalini, V., V. Dayakara Reddy, M. Srihari and Digumarti Bhaskara Rao (2004). *Vidya Adharalu (Foundations of Education)*. Guntur: Sri Nagarjuna Publishers.

Subba Rao, K.P., P. Ayodhya and Digumarti Bhaskara Rao (2004). *Patasala Yajamanyam-Vidhya Vyavasthalu (School Management and Systems of Education)*. Guntur: Sri Nagarjuna Publishers.

Sudhakar, V., B. Ravindra Babu, D.S. Kumar and Digumarti Bhaskara Rao (2004). *Vidya Sanketika Sastram-Computer Vidya (Educational Technology and Computer Education)*. Guntur: Sri Nagarjuna Publishers.

Index

H

I

J

K

L

M

Q

R